# Crash Course in Library Services
# to Preschool Children

**Recent Titles in Libraries Unlimited**
**Crash Course Series**

# Crash Course in Library Services to Preschool Children

**Betsy Diamant-Cohen**

**Crash Course Series**

AN IMPRINT OF ABC-CLIO, LLC
Santa Barbara, California • Denver, Colorado • Oxford, England

**Library of Congress Cataloging-in-Publication Data**

Diamant-Cohen, Betsy.
  Crash course in library services to preschool children / Betsy Diamant-Cohen.
     p. cm.
  Includes bibliographical references and index.
  ISBN 978-1-59884-688-1 (pbk : alk. paper) 1. Libraries and preschool
  children—United States. I. Title.
  Z718.2.U6.D53 2010
  027.62'5—dc22          2010024071

ISBN: 978-1-59884-688-1

14 13 12 11 10   1 2 3 4 5

This book is also available on the World Wide Web as an eBook.
Visit www.abc-clio.com for details.

Libraries Unlimited
An Imprint of ABC-CLIO, LLC

ABC-CLIO, LLC
130 Cremona Drive, P.O. Box 1911
Santa Barbara, California 93116-1911

This book is printed on acid-free paper ∞
Manufactured in the United States of America

# Contents

# Acknowledgments

To my mom, who inspired my love of public libraries by telling stories about her roller-skating adventures on the marble floors of the children's room at the Ferguson Public Library in Stamford, Connecticut.

To Mrs. Bernice Shulman, my fifth-grade teacher, who allowed my best friend, Gail Grandy, and I, to use our spare time to work as pages in the library of our elementary school.

To my dad who, when I was a teenager looking for my first job, told me that "the first job you get will reflect what you do for the rest of your life." I chose to work as a page in my local library.

To Charlotte Lesser from the Monmouth County Public Library system who hired me for my first job as a children's librarian and taught me how to hold books during storytimes.

To Claudia Homoki who taught me "Alligator, Alligator."

To Mary Handel who taught me all I ever wanted to know (and more!) about cataloging picture books.

To J.E.L.L.Y. (Jerusalem English Language Library for Youth) for hiring me as a roving storytime lady and providing many opportunities for creative programming.

To Sonia Moyd and Felecia Diggs for being great teammates while we were at the Exploration Center together.

To Blanche for asking me to write this book.

To Stuart for encouraging me to write this book.

To Yoella, who told me this book was "actually interesting!"

To Fran Glushakow-Gould and Deborah Margolis for help with proofreading and organization.

To Melanie Hetrick, for MUSTIE.

To Jennifer Cogan O'Leary for craft ideas that are ideal for two year olds.

To Regina Wade, for her Terrific Twos ideas, professional inspiration, and friendship.

To all my wonderful colleagues for sharing programming ideas, book recommendations, and enthusiasm for children's librarianship.

# Introduction

I have been a children's librarian for more than 20 years and have loved every minute of it. I have worked in a tiny township library where I was sometimes the children's librarian and the adult reference librarian at the same time; in a large suburban public library where I was part of a large staff; in a small town library where I was the entire children's department; in a large urban library system with many, many branches; in a museum library; and in a school library. I have worked as a children's librarian in county systems, in city systems, for a small town, in a child-care center, and as an independent traveling "storytime" librarian. I have presented storytimes and puppet shows inside libraries, next to swimming pools, at picnic tables, in shopping malls, in countless schools and child-care facilities, in prisons, in homeless shelters, in museums, and in hospitals.

I have run countless summer reading programs with themes that included music, gorillas, outer space, sports, and mysteries. In one library, I had to make my own flyers (graphics included—so the flyers did not look particularly professional). In another library, graphic requests for any printed material had to be submitted for approval and were created by a specific department. In another library, the children's department had its own graphic artist who could design and create logos, illustrations for flyers, and flannel board pieces whenever they were requested.

Each library had its own special style of doing things that was shaped by the clientele, the size of the library, and the library location. Although each place was different from the others, there were many similarities. These similarities are what I have chosen to highlight in this book. Clearly, the services that are offered time and time again, the policies that remain consistent from place to place, the traditions that are respected everywhere—these are the things that make up children's librarianship.

Thus, for a crash course in preschool library services, it makes sense to write about the similarities. No two libraries will do everything the same way, but based on my experiences, I believe these are the things that make up the essence of preschool services in public libraries. However, this opinion is based on my experiences; for another librarian, the content of a crash course in preschool services might be very different indeed.

Children's librarianship is a noble job, and working with the under-five crowd can be rewarding and exhausting at the same time. Children's librarians working with preschoolers are often underpaid, but that in no way diminishes the importance of their jobs. Children's librarians have the opportunity to work with children from birth to the age of five as well as with their parents or caregivers. Because the brain develops most rapidly during the earliest years of life and experiences actually help to form the architecture of the brain, it is imperative that children have at least one warm and loving relationship with a parent or caregiver. The librarian might not be the person to hold that very special role. However, librarians can use public library programs to teach adults about the special place in their young children's lives, encouraging them to interact with their children in ways that make their relationship a closer, more communicative one. A change like that could make the difference in a child's school career as well as in her self-esteem and ability to make correct judgments in difficult situations.

Children's librarianship for preschoolers may be tiring, stressful, and crazy. One day you may be wracking your brain trying to find books on an obscure topic for a four year old who has developed an interest in a specific topic while his mother insistently asks for all the books in the world on that topic to read to him. Another day, you may be faced with a class of 45 preschoolers who descend on your library and start going wild while their teachers sit down at the computers and begin checking their e-mail, totally ignoring the children. You may tussle with unattended adults who want to hang out in the children's room and feel it is their right as taxpayers to do so, or children who want to stay on the computer ALL DAY LONG! You may be administering a summer reading program for a group of 100 children or 10,000 children.

Whatever you do, I hope this crash course in preschool librarianship will help by providing a quick manual to guide you through the myriad responsibilities in this incredible job. You will be affecting lives and making a real difference, even if none of your visitors admits to the importance of the public library in their lives. Your salary might not be huge, but the impact you have on your community might be. For choosing this noble profession, I salute you!

# CHAPTER 1

# Overview of Children's Services to Preschoolers in Public Libraries

This chapter identifies preschoolers and the adults who care for them, provides an overview of the services to be offered to preschoolers and their parents and caregivers, and details the job responsibilities of the preschool librarian. Suggestions are given for providing resources on parenting in the children's area and information on child development and school readiness.

## Who Are Preschoolers?

The term "preschoolers" refers to children who have not yet entered elementary school. These children may or may not be in a child-care setting, they may or may not be able to read, and they may or may not have had the opportunity to play with children their own age.

Preschoolers can usually speak well enough to make their needs known; they have opinions, and they can run, hop, and jump without needing an adult to hold on to. They are capable of rolling a ball, catching a ball. They may or may not have the confidence to sit in a library program either with or without an adult. They should have the motor skills that enable them to turn book pages without ripping them. They may

1

be familiar with their letters, or they may not. They may have favorites: favorite colors, foods, animals, songs, and books. In the United States, children are often out of diapers by age three, but not necessarily.

The audiences for preschool library programs are typically divided into three categories. "Babies" or "Infants" often refer to children from birth to age two, although this can be broken down into further designations of "nonwalkers" and "walkers." "Toddlers" refers to two year olds or children who have just discovered their walking feet and are not yet steady on their feet but find it incredibly difficult to keep still; and "preschoolers" usually refers to children from ages three to five.

## Who Are the Adults?

A librarian working with preschoolers must realize that the parents of the preschoolers or their caregivers are also important clients. Unless the library is within close walking distance and there are no streets to cross, the adults are responsible for bringing their children to the library. They are the ones who generally hold onto the library card and who remind the child when it is time to bring books back to the library. They keep track of the calendar and know which days are "library days." If preschoolers lack the verbal skills to ask for what they want or what they are interested in, the adult can often serve as a spokesperson for the child.

Because children mimic their caregiving adult, it is important for the adults attending library programs to be fully involved. At the beginning of all programs, it helps to mention that children mimic the adults that they love. "For your child to get the most out of this program, it is important for you to be fully involved. Turn off your cell phones, know that there will be plenty of time to talk with your friends after the program, and during the next 30 minutes, try to be as involved as you can. Join in the songs, perform the fingerplays with gusto, and play your musical instruments with cheerful abandon. If your child sees you enjoying your participation, he or she will get the most out of the program." This solves two problems: it explains to the adult why their active participation is necessary, and it also establishes the "no cell phones" policy without having to present it as a restrictive rule.

## Children's Services to Preschoolers in Public Libraries

A children's librarian can provide many services to preschoolers. Librarians can help find age-appropriate books for children (and their caregivers). They can provide educational and entertaining programs. They can provide a place with a warm and welcoming atmosphere for children and their families to visit. They can provide free computer resources and use library rules as a way to introduce young children to the types of behavior that are expected in public places. They can be nonjudgmental, knowledgeable adults who are available to listen to any question a child might have and provide an answer. They can be a resource for adults who want to learn how to be good parents and a resource for other adults such as child-care workers. Children's librarians provide materials for centers and model book sharing, dialogic reading, giving positive reinforcement, and storytelling. The children's librarian can be the goofy person who dresses up like a princess for Halloween or the helpful support providing books on loss when a family loses a young sibling to crib death. The children's librarian can fill the role of friend, teacher, and liaison to both preschoolers and their families.

## Overall Job Responsibilities

Services to the public that a preschool librarian can provide include:

- alerting families to all public library services, including how to get library cards, upcoming events

- answering directional questions

- presenting programs to the public

- running Summer Reading Clubs

- offering reference help and reader's advisory

- serving as a community resource by knowing about local child-care agencies, support agencies for children with special needs, and contact information for agencies that provide medical or any kind of emergency help

- answering telephone or e-mail queries

- ordering books through interlibrary loan for library visitors when requested

- presenting programs for visiting child-care center classes

- performing outreach programming for child-care centers

In addition to serving the public, preschool librarians are often expected to:

- maintain a collection of books, books on tape, CDs, and possibly DVDs or toys (This can include ordering, shelving, and weeding.)

- provide staffing of a specially designated space for children within the public library

- create contact and maintain lines of communication with local child-care centers, health clinics, YMCAs and other agencies that serve young children

- suggest and arrange for outside performers

- help out in other areas of the library when needed

## Atmosphere

A children's librarian needs to know many things to do the best job possible. There are technical skills, policies, resources, and practical tips that can make the job of a children's librarian easy. But the most important thing that a children's librarian can do is be friendly. Welcome people with a warm "Hello": walking into a new place is a bit disconcerting for everyone. Young children don't always know how to behave and very rarely can stay still and be perfectly quiet. Giving everyone who enters the Children's Room a warm welcome to set them at ease tells them that the librarian is glad they have come to visit the library. Friendly relations with all family members and caregivers are essential!

## Adults as Clients

By being warm and welcoming and creating relationships with the adults who are responsible for the preschoolers visiting the library, children's librarians improve their relationship with the children as well as with the entire family. This welcoming atmosphere is essential for a number of reasons; if a friendly rapport has been established with the adult, when a child begins running or yelling in the library, you can comfortably ask the child to use library manners without worrying about offending the family.

The children's librarian can serve as a valuable community resource for families with preschoolers. For instance, if a child comes to the library with an obvious untreated skin infection and the caregiver mentions that the family does not have medical insurance, the librarian can direct the family to emergency rooms that treat people without insurance. The librarian may provide similar referrals for special needs issues such as speech development and hearing. Preschoolers are not able to manage their own health care or finances; because caregivers are responsible for the preschoolers, it is essential for the children's librarian to maintain friendly contact with the adults as well as the children. When a family is in need, if the adults feel that the children's librarian is their ally, they may ask for help, and the librarian can use information about the community, about organizations, and about programs available for families in need to assist these parents.

Because it may be difficult to take a preschooler into the adult section of the library and spend time quietly browsing through bookshelves, many children's librarians have found it helpful to have books on parenting physically located in the children's room. For more about this, see the section "Parenting Collections" in Chapter 3.

In addition, the children's librarian may keep on hand a list of certified preschools in the area. A list of local places to visit with a preschooler may be useful if the library is located in a city that often has out-of-town visitors. Caregivers also often appreciate lists of child-friendly restaurants.

# Child Development

Librarians are in the unique position of being able to observe many preschoolers. If a parent or caregiver is concerned about a youngster's development, early assessment is the best way to both diagnose and fix potential problems. Some developmental problems can be fixed if recognized and treated by a certain young age.

For instance, particular vision problems can be easily corrected if treated while the child is still young. If unnoticed and untreated while the child is still a toddler, the brain may adapt by considering that a permanent condition. Even if the child receives physical therapy or surgery to physically correct the problem later in life, because the architecture of the brain has already been formed with the understanding that the child has certain vision problems, they will not be able to be corrected. "Lazy eye" or amblyopia is when one eye is stronger than another, resulting in the brain ignoring images from the weaker eye, and "crossed eyes" are caused by weak eye muscles and result in eyes that don't align in the same direction. Both of these conditions are noticeable in young children and can be treated at an early age. If the caregiver does not realize that treatment is an important option, the librarian can use friendly conversation to drop hints about the importance of early intervention and to provide information about the particular eye condition. Having material on hand that lists free services provided by local agencies is another way the librarian can assist.

If a caregiver approaches the librarian with serious concerns about the child's language development, hearing, or sight, the librarian can urge the caregiver to see the child's pediatrician as soon as possible. On the other hand, if a caregiver seems worried because the child is not doing exactly what the other children are doing, it helps to remind the parent that all children develop at different stages. Although there may be children who are able to read before they enter kindergarten, this is the exception rather than the rule. Some parents may be overachievers and request your assistance in helping their preschooler learn to read. It is important to reassure these caregivers that the most important way for their preschooler to develop is through play and playful activities. Pressuring preschoolers to respond to flash cards and to read before they are ready can be stressful and counterproductive. Rather than fostering a love of learning, it may leave them with a distaste for books. Joyful interactions that encourage exploration and play are the key to developmental learning for preschoolers.

## Early Literacy

An important job of the children's librarian is to help preschoolers develop early literacy skills. Attainment of proficient literacy is connected with successful functioning in society. Current research suggests that adult levels of literacy are a direct outgrowth of preliteracy and emergent literacy skills. Positive preschool experiences have been connected to higher rates of graduation from high school, higher levels of pay, more success at staying in long-term relationships, and lower rates of incarceration. Studies have translated these results into economic benefits suggesting that for every $1 spent on high-quality preschool education, somewhere between $14 and $17 is saved on adult prison stays. Further investigation has determined that this disparity is due to the acquisition of "school readiness skills," which help a child succeed in school.

## School Readiness

School readiness skills are the skills children should have when they enter kindergarten in order to be "ready to learn." A ready-to-learn child knows how to do things independently and can enter a social and educationally based environment relatively easily. Children who enter school with these skills have an easier time and are generally much more successful than those who do not have them. The five main domains of school readiness skills include social and emotional development, approaches to learning, cognition and general knowledge, physical well-being and motor development, and language development.

1.  Social and Emotional Development. These skills include:

    a.  *Self-confidence.* Children who have a strong sense of self are not afraid to ask questions when they do not understand something, are willing to stick up for themselves, and are willing to try new challenges because they believe that they have a good chance at succeeding. With a sufficient vocabulary, these children are able to express thoughts, listen and ask questions, and speak with others. They can work independently as well as with others.

    b.  *Self-regulation.* Children who have good self-regulation skills are able to think before they act. Even if they are angry, they will express anger with words rather than by hitting. These children will be able to listen to others and to follow directions. Being able to take turns and to wait patiently are all part of self-regulation.

    c.  *Sensitivity to others.* Attitude toward attending school can be greatly influenced by whether a child has friends there. Children learn very quickly to stay away from the child who is a bully or the child who makes fun of others. Children who enter kindergarten without understanding how to play and work with others may be branded negatively, and this label may stick with them throughout their school career. Entering school and knowing how to share toys, to play with others, to compromise, and to share the limelight sets the stage for positive social relationships with other children.

2.  Approaches to Learning

    a.  If a child has been exposed to books in a cheerful environment, he or she will have positive feelings about books and reading. A child who has attended preschool storytime at the library has already been in a classroom-type situation with a "leader/teacher" at the front giving directions and everyone else following along. This child will enter the classroom with a sense of familiarity with the structure and with a predisposition to interact positively with the teacher.

    b.  A child who has been exposed to many things, such as books, musical instruments, art materials, puppets, songs, dances, and games, will have a sense of familiarity with them if they are present in the kindergarten classroom. If the child has been encouraged to explore objects and books in a playful manner in the preschool years, this delightful sense of inquiry will carry over into kindergarten. On the other hand, if a child has been in a home where he or she has always been told to "be quiet" and "stop asking questions," that child may enter the kindergarten classroom trying to be as invisible as possible. Opportunities for exploration may be unrecognized if the child has been conditioned to think that self-preservation means remaining as quiet and as unobtrusive as possible.

    c.   A child who is ready for school is curious, active, and wants to learn.

3.   Cognition and General Knowledge

    a.   It is expected that children will enter school knowing certain facts. Being able to recognize patterns, to name colors, to sing commonly known songs along with classmates helps the child fit into the kindergarten classroom.

    b.   Understanding relationships can also be an important base for beginning school; for instance, children will have an easier time in kindergarten if they understand that the teacher should be called "Miss Susan" and greeted with a respectful "hello" rather than calling her "Teach" and greeting her with words that are not polite to use in public.

    c.   Although the kindergarten child may not know how to read or add, it helps if he or she is aware that there are visual representations for sounds and numbers.

    d.   Familiarly with games makes it easier for a child to play with others. Knowing the rules of a game and playing fairly are important to kindergarten children.

4.   Physical Well-Being and Motor Development

    a.   Children with vision problems are not able to see a blackboard; glasses may be required for a student to see what is happening in class.

    b.   Hearing aids may be necessary for a child who is hard of hearing.

    c.   Fine and gross motor skills help children hold pencils and use scissors.

    d.   Malnutrition can be responsible for the inability to pay attention or for excessive tiredness. A rumbling stomach can interfere with learning. A child who is not hungry all the time will find it easier to learn and retain information.

5.   Language Development

    a.   Having a store of vocabulary words means that a child will have the means for expressing himself. With words, a child can ask a question, express a concern, answer a question, give comfort to others, and tell a story. Without vocabulary, these activities can be difficult. A ready-to-learn child will be able to use a growing vocabulary.

b.  Understanding that words are composed of sounds (phonological awareness) is a first step to reading. Being able to hear the sounds (syllables) in words helps children in decoding and spelling. Being aware of language and written words and understanding how words are put together are important parts of language and literacy.

c.  Being experienced with and excited about books sets the scene for developing language and literacy skills. Familiarity with page-turning behavior, having a sense that English is read from left to right, and possessing a positive attitude about reading are basic school readiness skills.

d.  Pictures can tell stories. A child who has been exposed to picture books knows to look at the illustrations as well as to listen to the story. Visual literacy is when a child can use illustrations to decode a story or to provide supplemental information, thus "reading" the pictures.

Because school readiness skills can lead to success at school and in social relationships, gainful employment, and good citizenship, fostering these skills fits into the social mission of the public library.

## Reading Readiness

Literacy as a cognitive skill is largely connected to the development of the brain. Based on what we now know about reading, readiness to read is often considered almost as important as literacy itself. Research tells us that early literacy in the form of reading readiness is based on the following skills:

- Letter knowledge

- Narrative skills (being able to tell a story)

- Phonological awareness (awareness of syllables)

- Print awareness (awareness of connections between written symbols and words)

- Print motivation (a positive attitude toward books)

- Vocabulary

Handouts in English and Spanish on the six early literacy skills are available on the Web site of the Idaho Commission for Libraries: http://libraries.idaho.gov/page/read-to-me-resources.

## Early Literacy Programs

Programs such as Every Child Ready to Read @ your library are designed to help children develop the necessary preliteracy skills that will help them be successful at school. Recognition of the important role played by each child's caregiver is an essential component of this program. Caregivers are encouraged to use dialogic reading with their children, asking questions about the stories or giving the children opportunities to tell stories about the illustrations or stories. The official Web site for Every Child Ready to Read @ your library (ECRR) can be found at http://www.ala.org/ala/mgrps/divs/alsc/ecrr/index.cfm.

*Early Literacy Storytimes @ Your Library: Partnering with Caregivers for Success* by Saroj Ghoting and Pamela Martin-Diaz (ALA Editions, 2005) gives practical programming suggestions for children under the age of five. ECRR Family Workshop scripts, developed by Saroj Ghoting, are available at http://www.earlylit.net/readytoread/indexE.htm#scripts. The Johnson County Library in Kansas has a special early literacy center and hosts a Web site with reading readiness information based partially on ECRR including a list of recommended books, videos of fingerplays, and wordless books at http://www.jocolibrary.org/6by6.

## Librarians and Child-Care Providers

Information about reading readiness such as the importance of child–adult bonding, exposure to books, and dialogic reading is important for child-care providers as well as for parents and guardians. Some libraries offer training workshops for local child-care providers based on ECRR, facilitated by the children's librarians.

Public libraries can use what is currently known about brain research to help create optimal learning environments for their children's programs. The next chapter discusses the elements necessary for such programs.

## More about the Caregivers

A librarian working with preschoolers must realize that the parents of the preschoolers, or their caregivers, are also important clients. While preschoolers benefit from storytime, their caregivers may also reap a number of benefits. The children hear the stories, they see the illustrations, they may be involved in gross or fine motor activity, and they may sing songs or recite rhymes along with the librarian. They are exposed to books and illustrations in a warm and nurturing setting. It is hoped that they will develop a positive connection with books and an enthusiastic reaction to books that will follow them into kindergarten helping to shape their attitude of joy and curiosity when they enter elementary school.

The adults in the programs, however, can also derive great benefit. By inserting developmental tips into the program, librarians can actually use storytime as an opportunity to educate the adults. A developmental tip is a short phrase spoken by the librarian while presenting a program that is meant to educate the adults in the audience. Developmental tips can address different topics and can provide ideas, inspiration, and education to caregivers present at the preschool program. For example, tips can

- explain something about a child's development, for instance, "Children this age don't sit perfectly still."

- explain the value of an activity. For instance, "Playing freeze games conditions children to instantly respond to the word "stop."

- give parents ideas for activities that can be replicated at home. For instance, "Ask your children to tap their name on pots and pans, and then go around the house tapping the names of objects on the upside down pot. This helps children hear the sounds in words (called phonological awareness), which is an important precursor to reading."

- offer a chance to publicize your role as a community resource. If a parent has expressed concern that his or her preschooler is not responding to activities in the same way as other children, you may use a development tip to publicize Infant and Toddler Assessment Centers or other local agencies where free assessments of a child's development are available.

- provide suggestions for activities. For instance, "While taking a walk with your child, encourage conversation. Count how many trees you see, ask your child to describe a particular flower, or ask your child to point out any signs and then read them aloud. Casual conversation with a close adult is an easy way to help children develop their vocabularies."

- Connect specific books with activities that are replicable at home. For instance, after reading a version of "Goldilocks and the Three Bears," a tip might encourage adults to make oatmeal with their children and talk about the connection between oatmeal and porridge.

By being warm and welcoming and creating relationships with the adults who are responsible for preschoolers visiting the library, the children's librarian improves his or her relationship with the children.

Because librarians have had difficulty finding a wide variety of appropriate developmental tips for their weekly toddler programs, I created a set of developmental tip cards with my colleague Saroj Ghoting that provides 102 tips, along with related activities and resources, called *The Early Literacy Kit: A Handbook and Tip Cards* (ALA Editions, 2009).

## Resources for the Preschool Librarian

In addition to the wide assortment of books and Web sites that list good books and program ideas for preschoolers, there is a wonderful resource that is always at your fingertips: your colleagues! Librarians love helping each other. And, if you're facing a problem, it is logical to assume that the same problem has confronted another children's librarian before you. One of the best ways to figure out what to do is to learn how other librarians have solved the same problem. If your state library has a children's library consultant, you might contact that person.

Joining a professional organization of children's librarians is one way to meet colleagues. Most states have state library organizations; many have special divisions for children's librarians. On a national level, the American Library Association has a division for children's librarians called ALSC (Association for Library Service to Children). ALSC members receive a newsletter called "ALSConnect" that highlights successful programming ideas and good resources, lists division activities, and provides helpful information for librarians working with children. The ALSC blog can be found at http://www.alsc.ala.org/blog. The ALSC listserv can be found at: http://lists.ala.org/wws/info/alsc-l.

A number of other helpful listservs for preschool librarians are available. PubYac (PUBlic libraries, Young Adults, and Children) is a listserv for librarians serving children and youth in public libraries. Children's librarians often write into PubYac with "stumpers" (a question that a library visitor has asked regarding a specific book that they are looking for), and the "collective brain" of the listserv provides the answer. Fellow librarians good-naturedly answer questions about ideas for storytimes on a particular theme, share recommendations of good places for purchasing puppet theatres, talk about their experiences with Summer Reading Performers, and compare notes on computer stations. All questions regarding children's librarianship are welcome. This is a great way for a librarian in a small, isolated community to benefit from the experience and knowledge of her peers. You can subscribe at http://www.pubyac.org/index.html.

ALSC sponsors an online Preschool Services Discussion Group, which also has open meetings at every national ALA Conference. You can subscribe at http://lists.ala.org/wws/info/preschsvcs. Other ALSC discussion groups that might be of interest are the Children and Technology Interest Group, whose wiki can be found at http://wikis.ala.org/alsc/index.php/ALSC_ChildTech_Wiki; the Storytelling Discussion Group; and the Children's Book Discussion Group. Childlit is a listserv for children's literature. To subscribe to the children's literacy discussion forum, send an e-mail to child_lit@mailman.rutgers.edu, with "Subscribe Child_lit" in the subject line. To subscribe to a children's and young adult's literature listserv, send an e-mail to listserv@bingvmb.cc.binghamton.edu, with "Subscribe KIDLIT-L" in the subject line.

Library Success: A Best Practices Wiki can be found at http://www.libsuccess.org/index.php?title=Main_Page and information about the Kids @ Your Library Campaign can be found at http://wikis.ala.org/alsc/index.php/Kids!_@_your_library_Best_Practices_Wiki.

# Summary

Public library services to preschoolers encompass services for children under the age of five as well as services to their parents, guardians, and child-care providers. There are many resources that can help with different aspects of each type of service. Because librarians enjoy sharing information, whether you are in a small or large library, one of your best resources can be your colleagues.

# CHAPTER 2

## Programming

A successful library program requires good content, well-formed structure, and an enthusiastic manner of delivery. It must take place in an environment created with children in mind. The ideal preschool program is one that incorporates scientific findings into practice in as many ways as possible while remaining age appropriate for the age three to five crowd. Ideal programs are ones that encourage development of school readiness skills, promote bonding between parents and their children, and enrich children's lives through the arts. They also take multiple intelligences into account by providing experiences for different kinds of learners including visual learners, kinesthetic learners, linguistic learners, and musical learners.

A good library program for preschoolers introduces them joyfully into the world of books and stories. It stimulates imagination, builds vocabulary, and inspires ideas. Looking at illustrations helps children develop a sense of beauty and color. Interacting with other children in library programs gives the opportunity to practice patience and turn-taking as well as to develop social skills. Children experience being part of a group, they learn how to listen and follow directions, and they understand at a very young age their value as part of a community.

# Scheduling

Most early literacy programs get the largest audiences on weekday or weekend mornings. Some librarians have success with afternoon programs, but if a family has older children who are finished with school by that time, the opportunity for private parent–child time together in a library program is lost. In addition, nap times and mealtimes need to be taken into consideration. Most librarians agree that 10:30 A.M. is the best time for a preschool program in the library. Some librarians have experimented with running evening programs that enable working parents to attend with their children. Depending on your community, this may or may not be successful.

# Programming Elements

To have the best preschool program possible for young children, the program should have a number of elements in it: song, rhymes, movement, play, exposure to book illustration, repetition, and ritual. The atmosphere should be one in which everyone feels safe and comfortable. Preschoolers like to know what to expect, so it is helpful to follow the same format from program to program. It is reassuring to a child to know how each program starts and ends; opening and closing rituals help with this.

## Songs

Learning and singing songs is an easy way for children to build up a vocabulary while helping them to incorporate patterns of speech and voice inflection. Exposure to music through song helps them develop artistically, socially, and emotionally. Singing together creates community. Lullabies provide stress relief and can be used as a relaxation technique. The human voice is a wonderful, natural musical instrument to incorporate. Singing does not require financial outlay, technical skill, or fancy equipment. Including sing-a-long songs in programs provides preschoolers with opportunities to sing along with the group, to exercise their memories, to develop their use of vocabulary words, and to build their participation in the storytime community. Repeatedly singing the same songs gives participants a repertoire of songs to sing together.

Preschoolers have short attention spans; the inclusion of songs or fingerplays in between read-aloud stories helps children from becoming restless. The change of pace helps them to stretch cramped muscles and keeps them alert for the next story.

A great resource for librarians and teachers who want to use music in programming but who think that they have no musical ability is Regina Carlow's *Exploring the Connection Between Children's Literature and Music* (Libraries Unlimited, 2008).

## Repetition

Not many librarians are professional singers. It is useful to repeat the same songs from week to week, so participants can learn the songs and sing along with you. If you use new songs all the time, the program becomes a musical performance rather than a community sing-a-long. And what would library visitors rather do, come to a place each week to hear a musical performance by someone who is not a professional singer, or participate in a community sing-a-long with songs with which both they and their children are familiar?

In addition, when young children like a book, they will often ask their parents to read it over and over again. Each time they hear the same story, they get pleasure out of it and learn something new from it. Young children enjoy knowing what to expect and eagerly anticipate each step of the story. It is useful for librarians to learn from this and not be afraid to repeat books in their programs. Although there is a rich world of books, with new ones being published on a regular basis, reading aloud the same age-appropriate books with children is an educationally sound practice.

## Movement

Children love to move. It is not unusual for a child who is sitting to get the wiggles long before an adult might feel the need to move a bit. Building movement activities into programs uses this propensity to move to your advantage. In addition to always having some sort of standing-up rhymes in programs, movement can also be used to foster imagination. For instance, some preschool storytimes begin when the children are asked to stand in a line with their hands on the shoulders of the person in front of them and to pretend to be a train chugging into the storytime room together. Movement can also be used to mimic the actions of different animals or to recreate parts of a story.

Preschoolers enjoy movement songs such as "Head, Shoulders, Knees, and Toes" as well as "The Hokey Pokey." They like physical challenges such as going faster and faster until it becomes difficult. Freeze games where children move to recorded music and then are asked to freeze whenever the music stops are often popular. Some popular CDs that require listening to the songs and following the actions are *Jim Gill Makes It Noisy in Boise, Idaho* by Jim Gill and *Big Fun* by Greg and Steve.

These can be purchased online at Jim Gill's online store (http://store.jimgill.com/cd2.html), at Greg and Steve's online store (http://www.gregandsteve.com/store.php), or at Amazon.com.

## Musical Instruments

In her book *Scientist in the Crib,* Alison Gopnick asserts that all young children are scientists trying to make sense of their world. Their whole life is making hypotheses and then testing them out. Even at a very young age, they put things in their mouths because they don't just want to know how something looks; they also want to find out how it feels and tastes. Providing children with different types of rhythm instruments is a great way to encourage their scientific inquiry, teaching them about cause and effect ("if I shake the bell, it will ring; if I hold the bell still, it will not make noise"). Basic percussion instruments are easy and fun to play; they can also help to promote early literacy skills and make connections in the brain.

A young child will learn to look at an instrument and know through experience how to play it (ring, shake, tap, etc.) as well as what type of noise it will make. Use the different vocabulary words for each instrument; that is, *tap* the sticks together, *ring* the bell, *shake* the maraca, or *hit* the drum. Encouraging children to experiment by playing slowly, quickly, softly, loudly, up high, down low, in a circle and from side-to-side expands their vocabulary as well as their musical and spatial awareness.

Playing recorded music while asking group participants to play along with their instruments is a way to help children develop listening skills. It is also a great way to expose them to many types of music. Rather than just using children's songs, include selections from classical music, rock and roll, bluegrass, reggae, country, and others. Each type of music has its own particular flavor and beat. The best type of music for this activity does not have to be specifically written or geared for children; it simply needs to have a steady beat. On a practical level, play on rhythm instruments in the library can be translated into playing with pots, pans, and kitchen utensils at home.

## Play

Learning in the context of play has many rich benefits. Happy experiences are ones people like to remember. By incorporating play into your preschool programs, you will be creating a happy experience. Play enables children to experiment. Passing out musical instruments and giving children time to play and experiment with them gives children a way to spark their curiosity to find out on their own about the properties of a thing. This type of exploratory behavior may be replicated with other objects such as kitchen implements, colored scarves, and plastic animals.

Play can lead to social development. When two children play together, there is some type of social interaction. Perhaps sharing or turn-taking will be involved. Social play helps children develop problem-solving skills by enabling them to act out different scenarios in a safe way until they find the one that feels right to them. They learn empathy by literally being able to put themselves in someone else's shoes. Social play builds attachments between children that can develop into friendships. Physical play is a great way to help children develop both fine and gross motor skills. Within the library, physical play can be encouraged through movement activities. Push toys, building blocks, puzzles, and wooden maze games all assist with the development of motor skills. These may be incorporated into programs or be available for free play both before and after programs.

Integrating play into programs is also a way to model positive play behavior for parents. In the group setting, parents can watch how other parents interact with their children. They might observe the librarian sitting on the floor doing a puzzle with some children. The caregiving adults can see how play can be a natural, fun, shared experience. Some parents mistakenly believe that the best way to encourage their child's cognitive development is to constantly provide intellectual stimulation by reading aloud; discussing everything under the sun while always using sophisticated vocabulary words; encouraging preschoolers to memorize letters, numbers, and words; and using flashcards. However, research indicates that play is the best learning experience for all young children. Lack of play can put children at a real disadvantage. Although teachers are trained to teach writing and mathematics, social skills, self-esteem, and emotional maturity are traits that children develop though their social interactions and experiences with others. Thus, play is essential for preschoolers, and by including play in programming, library programs can help develop early literacy and school readiness skills.

## Art as Visual Literacy

Learning how to look at artwork, to enjoy the visual experience, to understand that a picture of an object is a visual representation of an abstract concept or may be connected with the written word is one of the first steps of early literacy. Parents don't necessarily think of illustrations in books as artwork, and attention is often paid to the reading of the story rather than to discussing the illustrations. However, interest in illustration, learning how to look, and experiencing pleasure from looking at beautiful pictures is also part of early literacy skills. Giving children the knowledge that art can be used as a means to enjoyment may be giving a gift that will last their entire life. Parents may need to be clued in to the fact that looking together at book illustrations and talking about them with simple comments ("Look how much blue is used in this picture!" "This cow is bigger than that cow, and he has a longer tail.") can help children to increase their powers of observation and ability to communicate. In *Young Children and*

*Picture Books* (NAEYC, 2004), Mary Jalongo provides more information about preschoolers and book illustration.

## Ritual

Using a specific song or fingerplay to open or close a session every time is a great way to create a ritual that will be both meaningful and comforting. When a program always starts and ends with the same song, children know what to expect. By launching your program with a ritual, you are telling the children, "The program is about to begin, put yourself in program mode. It's going to be fun but it is going to require your attention and participation." Children feel safe when they know what to expect, and the ritual is one way to increase that sense of safety. You may notice that if you always start with one particular rhyme and then forget to use it another week, the children will all gleefully remind you that you have forgotten your ritual. "Hello songs," a short welcome speech delivered by a puppet mascot, a fingerplay, or a name game have all been used by children's librarians as opening rituals for preschool programs. An example of a ritual is provided later in this chapter.

## Registration versus Non-Registration

Some librarians require registration for programs. Advance registration for programs means that the librarian can have an approximate idea of how many children will be coming, how many supplies to prepare, what type of audience will be attending a program (preschoolers with parents or child-care centers where there is very low ratio of children to adults), and the exact ages of the audience. Registration may be available for one-time programs or for weekly happenings, such as preschool storytime.

### Preschool Storytime

Registration for preschool storytime generally happens when the library offers storytime in a series of six-week sessions with a two- or three-week break in between each series. In communities where the demand for preschool storytime exceeds space limits or librarian availability, registration may be the only way to safely and fairly accommodate the crowd. Although requiring registration gives the librarian a rough idea of how many participants will be at the sessions, it also means that attendance at the programs is limited. For this reason, many libraries try to avoid registration unless absolutely necessary.

Without registration, the librarian has to be prepared to receive all types of audiences. A program meant for 15 children may suddenly swell to an audience of 100. The librarian cannot turn people away, and so must always have an alternative plan in mind. Perhaps it may mean moving to a bigger program room, using books with larger illustrations, removing the craft component of the program (because not enough templates have been prepared), among others. Librarians running programs without registration must be prepared to think on their feet and deal with any situation that may arise by not knowing ahead of time exactly which ages and how many children will be coming to programs.

Registration is meant to guarantee an audience as well as to make sure that programs are not overcrowded. It can also be a deterrent to parents who realize that they can't possibly commit to bringing their preschooler every week for the next six weeks. A simple solution is to offer programs at the library at the same time every week with no registration and no breaks in between. This can become complicated when a librarian wants to go on vacation or just needs a one-week break from the programming. To avoid burnout in the librarians, find someone in the community who plays guitar to lead a community sing-a-long with well-known songs such as "The Eency Weency Spider" and "Old MacDonald Had a Farm" during the usual storytime slot. This helps to keep families involved while allowing the librarian some flexibility.

## Baby Programs

Some programs for babies run in six-week sessions and require registration, but this is not ideal. Babies can be very unpredictable, and it is counterproductive to require adults to register. Imagine this: a mother wants to attend lapsit programs (described in the next section) at the library, so she registers her child as soon as she hears a six-week session is about to start. She and her child have a wonderful time at the first program, and the mom is looking forward to the next five programs. One week later, she takes her child to the pediatrician for a checkup, and her baby receives an inoculation. The baby gets very cranky and does not stop crying. The mother realizes that it would not make sense to go to the library. The night before the third program, the baby is up all night teething, whining, and crying, and the mother is totally exhausted. She is determined to go the program at the library, and she puts her overtired child into the car seat. Just as they arrive at the library, the baby falls asleep. The mother realizes that if she moves her child, the baby will wake up, so instead she uses the quiet time in the car to catch up on her reading. Both mother and baby are ready to go to the fourth session at the library, but as they are about to walk out the door, the baby spits up all over herself. As soon as she is in a new, clean outfit, she has a bout of diarrhea which seeps through her diaper and soils her Babygro. Mom cheerfully changes her and heads out of the door again, and baby has another bowel movement. Mom gives up.

Mom and baby actually make it to the library for the fifth program and have a great time. By now, mom has "baby brain;" with the lack of sleep and so many things to carry around whenever she and baby go out, her memory is not what it used to be. When the sixth week rolls around, mom is not sure whether this is the last session or if the last session was the prior week. Rather than making a mistake and packing up the diaper bag, the wipes, the spare outfits, the bottle, the blanket, and taking baby down to the library only to find out that the program ended the prior week, mom decides to simply stay home. At the next library visit, mom is asked if she wants to register for the next series of six sessions. Although she enjoyed the program, she realizes that she can't possibly commit to coming each of the six weeks, and she doesn't want to take up a spot that someone else might use. So she does not register and therefore does not attend any more of the sessions. However, if programs for babies were offered at the library at the same time every week with no registration and no breaks in between, this mother and her child would most likely become frequent and happy participants. When planning your schedule, consider what will be best for your audience.

# Programming for Babies

Because programs for babies often involve having the child on the parent or caregiver's lap, they are often referred to as "lapsit" programs. They generally last between 15 and 30 minutes and involve rhymes and songs.

Obviously, babies and toddlers cannot attend a program on their own. In fact, library programs created for babies are best if they keep two things in mind: the developmental abilities of the baby and the needs of the adult.

Babies can be divided into two groups, the nonmobile and the mobile. Nonmobile babies sit in their parents' laps and watch as the adult performs. The parents help their children participate in the activities in a variety of ways, such as maneuvering their hands. Mobile babies may already have the physical dexterity to manipulate objects (such as a bell or scarf) on their own.

A library program for babies should involve singing, music, a warm and safe atmosphere, repetition, ritual, some type of book connection, opportunities for exploration, activities that encourage positive social interaction, exposure to words, and increased bonding with the caregiver. Babies do not have long attention spans, and it may seem as if they are not paying attention. Do not be discouraged; they are soaking up everything going on around them and, when the time comes, they will demonstrate what they have learned. Of course, you may have a baby who always falls asleep as soon as the program starts and stays sleeping throughout the whole thing. This is fine, because the caregiver is still coming and learning lots of beneficial activities to do with baby while they are together outside of the program. So encourage the caregiver to keep coming.

Instead or reading books aloud, model how to play with books. Sing songs about animal illustrations, show a picture from a book to illustrate a rhyme you are reciting, or show the cover of the book if the title is the same as a nursery rhyme you are about to recite. The message you will be getting across is that books can be used in many ways with very young children; reading them aloud to babies is best if the book is very short.

## Music in Baby Programs

Babies need songs that are short and simple to sing. They like the chance to experiment with different textures and objects such as colored scarves and bells. They need positive physical contact with their adult, so songs that involve hugging and gentle tickling are great. Lullabies can help to calm agitated babies. Bouncing to a steady beat reminds them of the heartbeat sounds when they were in their mother's womb, and they find it very comforting. So adding knee bounces such as "The Grand Old Duke of York" to any program for very young children is a good idea.

## Setting the Scene

You may want to begin your program by telling parents that children learn best by mimicking. They will get the most out of the program if their adult is fully participating. Thus, all cell phones should be turned off, and conversations between adults should wait until the program has finished. Also, tell parents that if a child starts to cry, it is fine with you if the parent takes them out of the room to calm down and then comes back once the child is comfortable. Rather than asking adults to take their child outside as if it were a punishment, explain that you are comfortable with people walking in and out of the programs, and you know that it is easier for a child to calm down when they are in a quieter setting. If you are using musical instruments, you may want to mention that children often explore by putting things in their mouths. When collecting the instruments, be sure to put the wet ones in a different place than the dry ones and pay extra attention to disinfecting them before the next session.

## Recommended Baby Programs

*Mother Goose on the Loose* is a 30-minute nursery rhyme-based program that I developed that seamlessly combines book illustration, musical instruments, vocabulary, games, songs, puppets, reading aloud, and nursery rhymes. The activities accompanying familiar songs and rhymes are designed to help children develop school readiness skills, socialization skills, and self-confidence. During the program, the librarian models reading a book aloud, playful behavior, giving positive reinforcement, and using books cheerfully without reading from them. Developmental tips are given informally during the program. *Mother Goose on the Loose* is based on the "Listen, Like, Learn" approach developed by Canadian music educator Barbara Cass-Beggs. It follows a structure and formula that make it very easy to plan on a weekly basis once the first program has been created. It uses best practices for learning by incorporating repetition, ritual, music, movement, and nurturing contact. It provides a framework for using a variety of musical instruments and props during programs. A complete manual with everything you need to know called *Mother Goose on the Loose: A Handbook and CD-ROM Kit with Scripts, Rhymes, Songs, Flannel-Board Patterns, and Activities* (Neal-Schuman, 2006) is available at http://www.neal-schuman.com/bdetail.php?isbn=1555705367.

Another recommended program is Every Child Ready to Read @ your library. Based on research on brain development and early literacy, this program was developed jointly by the Public Library Association and the Association for Library Service to Children. Information about research and evaluation, instructions for booking training workshops, and downloadable materials are available at http://www. ala.org/ala/mgrps/divs/alsc/ecrr/index.cfm.

## About Toddlers

Toddlers are generally children between the ages of 24 months and 36 months. Toddlers are a unique class of children. Often called "Terrible Twos" because of their love for saying "no" to almost everything, toddlers have a wonderful energy that pushes them to explore just about everything. They are constantly on the move physically and are experimenting with speech as well.

Two years olds find it difficult to stay still. They have just discovered their feet, and they want to move, move, move, move. One of the most important ways to begin library programs for toddlers is to let the caregivers know that "children this age don't sit perfectly still, and it's fine if they wander around." Delineate the area in which you are working and ask caregivers to physically take the child back if he or she walks into that space. This will put the caregiver at ease. They will not worry that their children are "misbehaving" if they wander, yet they will know what to do if their child starts grabbing your props or blocks the view of everyone else. By mentioning this fact of child development, you are also teaching adults not to have unrealistic expectations of their children. The result is an accepting atmosphere in which children feel free to explore and adults don't worry about other adults judging them based on their children's behavior. Although it may not seem as if the roaming toddlers are paying attention, they are actually absorbing most of what is going on around them.

Toddlers have limited attention spans for sitting and listening. Because of their developing cognitive skills, they are too old for baby programs, but because of their inability to sit and pay attention, they are not ready for preschool storytimes. They like looking at books, but not for too long. The best books for them are very short books with brief text and big pictures that are easy to see. Children this age enjoy books with which they can repeat a chorus or phrases with you, such as *Jump Frog, Jump.* They enjoy lift-the-flap books that allow them to shout out the name of the animal or object that suddenly appears. Concept books can be turned into a game if you point at an object and ask the children to name it or point to a number of objects and count them aloud together. Two year olds love showing off their knowledge! It helps them feel good about themselves and their intellect, it encourages them to enjoy learning, and it gives their caregiver an opportunity to feel proud of their child's progress. Building these opportunities into programs for toddlers is essential.

## About Toddler Programs

While toddler programs can last anywhere from 20 minutes to 45 minutes, they are usually only 30 minutes. To keep the children engaged, make sure that all books read aloud are very, very short. In between every book should be some type of activity: a puppet asking questions, a fingerplay, a song, an exercise, or playing with musical instruments. Be sure to have standing-up activities at least once so that children can move together as a group and get their wiggles out. The most successful toddler programs are those that are packed with activities and can seamlessly go from one thing to another with minimal waiting in between. In addition, toddlers love routine, so it is helpful to keep ritual and repetition as part of all your toddler programs.

## Programming Ideas for Toddlers

Two year olds benefit from experiencing books using many of their senses. For instance, *Rosie's Walk* (Hutchins, Macmillan, 1968) is a great book to use with toddlers. A hula hoop can become the pond, a chair can become a haystack, a chair with a bottle of honey on it can become the beehive, and a quick touch of some flour that has been placed in a bowl can represent the mill. Children can listen to the book and then actually take a walk around Rosie's farm. They can follow along with the actual text of the book while circling around the pond and climbing over the haystack. By walking around a room with "stations" for each of these activities, the children experience the book in a way that goes much deeper than merely listening to the story being read aloud and looking at the illustrations.

Regina Wade has many creative ideas for children this age including one for "The Three Little Kittens." Fill small plastic bins with a small amount of water; add some dish soap to one of the bins. Cut mitten shapes out of sheets of spongy material that expand in water and invite children to wash their mittens just as the three kittens did. First the children can "clean" their mittens in the soapy water. Then the mittens can be rinsed out in clear water. Finally the mittens can be squeezed thoroughly to remove all additional water, and they can be attached to a clothesline with come clothes pins. The rhyme could be recited again, and the children can be asked if the illustrations remind them of what they actually did with their mittens.

Jennifer Cogan O'Leary created a wonderful list of art activities for very young children including stringing Cheerios onto a pipe cleaner. Young children enjoy finger-painting on top of a Ziploc® plastic bag that has been sealed with paint inside. It is not messy but is still a fun tactile experience. They can color using large crayons, stick things together using glue sticks, and spread white glue with craft sticks. You are welcome to contact Jennifer if you'd like more ideas (jcogan98@yahoo.com).

Toddlers who are just learning to speak may enjoy filling in one word of a song. For instance, encourage parents to sing "Twinkle, twinkle little . . . ." Ask them to pause, and the child will most likely joyfully fill in "STAR." Tell parents that this is a wonderful achievement and encourage them to repeat activities such as these as the child matures. The children will remember more words and eventually proudly sing the entire song. Giving children opportunities to sing along with the group helps to exercise their memory, develop their use of vocabulary, and build participation in the storytime community.

## Siblings at Toddler Programs

Perhaps you have planned a program for two year olds. A mother comes with her two year old and her five year old, and a number of other parents come with their five year olds. The best way to handle the situation is to make sure you have enough books to read aloud that are of interest to older children and to also include at least one or two that are still suitable to the audience of your target ages.

## Resources for Toddlers

*Mother Goose Programs* (http://www.mothergooseprograms.org), developed by the Vermont Center for the Book, teach parents and providers ways to use picture books to help children develop scientific curiosity, mathematics, and literacy skills.

Their Web site provides book lists, sample programs, downloadable activity sheets, free articles, and readable summaries of research regarding child development and early literacy. An excellent resource for planning programs specifically for toddlers is *Storytimes for Two-Year-Olds* by Judy Nichols (ALA Editions, 2007).

# Preschool Storytime

While preschoolers benefit from storytime, their caregivers may also reap a number of benefits. The children hear the stories, they see the illustrations, they may be involved in gross or fine motor activity, and they may sing songs or recite rhymes along with the librarian. They are exposed to books and illustrations in a warm and nurturing setting. In this way, they will develop a positive connection with books and an enthusiastic reaction to them that will follow them into kindergarten, helping to shape their attitude of joy and curiosity when they enter elementary school.

## Format

The traditional format for a preschool storytime is to have a librarian sit on a chair or stool in front of a group of children and adults who are sitting on the floor. Parents with children under the age of two should be encouraged to sit with the child in their lap or physically close by; preschoolers may feel more independent and want to sit farther away from their parents. To ask children to sit nicely with legs crossed, use the magic formula: "criss-cross applesauce."

A small table next to the librarian can hold the pile of books to be read and display the ones already used. A plastic storage bin, a basket, or a bucket can be set beside or behind the librarian. Any puppets or distracting props can be dropped into the basket as soon as their use has finished; because they are out of sight and out of mind, they will not be distracting to the preschoolers.

## Modeling

During programs, the librarian can model a variety of behaviors for the adults, such as book reading, singing, giving positive reinforcement, and playing. The most important modeling is enjoying the company of the children and joyfully relating to the books used.

## Manner of Delivery

Even if you have been having a bad day, it is extremely important for you to present programs in a cheerful way. The librarian's attitude rubs off on the participants; if you look as if you are having a good time with almost no effort, your audience will also be inclined to have a good time. If you are warm and welcoming, your audience will feel wanted and appreciated; even if you have had a long day and would rather be in bed, it is important for your group to feel wanted. Enthusiasm breeds enthusiasm; the librarian's attitude will often be reflected by the program participants. So, at every program presented, it is important for the librarian to smile, to look at the children directly in the eyes, and to let everyone know that they are welcome participants in the program.

# Preschoolers as Older Siblings Attending Baby Programs

Programs for babies and toddlers are very different from programs for preschoolers. It is extremely important during programs for babies *not* to read books that are long, and the librarian may perhaps read only a few pages from one book. Preschoolers, however, have a longer attention span, and will quickly get bored if the program is too simple for them. What can a librarian do, then, if a parent brings both a baby and a preschool sibling to a program for babies?

Preschoolers can be asked to be helpers; mature preschoolers might assist by passing out and collecting musical instruments or colored scarves. Or keep a few stuffed animals in your programming collections, and if you see preschoolers in your baby programs, make it a point to introduce them to the animals before the program begins. Explain that the animal really wants to participate, but his mother is not at the library. Then, ask the preschooler to act as the animal's parent during the program. It is amazing to see how seriously the preschoolers take to the task of bouncing the stuffed animals during the knee bounces, doing fingerplays with them, and even rocking them during a lullaby. This keeps the preschoolers focused by enabling them to be the caregiver for the animals; mommy or daddy is then free to interact with baby during the baby program.

# Planning a Preschool Storytime

A preschool storytime is a popular library program for preschoolers. It typically lasts for 30 minutes and follows a traditional form. It begins with a welcoming ritual and a brief introduction to the program. Then there is a combination of times to listen and activity times. A closing helps with the transition out of preschool storytime.

Although originally designed for infants and toddlers, *Mother Goose on the Loose* activities can be easily separated and inserted on a piecemeal basis into preschool storytime. Adapted versions of *Mother Goose on the Loose* geared for families with children from birth to age 5, also have rich offerings for preschoolers. In addition to the original program, there is a version in Spanish. *Early Literacy Programming en Español: Mother Goose on the Loose Programs for Bilingual Learners* (Diamant-Cohen, Neal-Schuman, 2010) provides step-by-step instructions for the non-Spanish-speaking librarian on how to create and offer high-quality programs for the Spanish-speaking community. It includes tips on finding a Spanish-speaking community partner, explains how to work together with that partner in developing and presenting programs, describes ways to create a welcoming environment in the library for this specific population, lists books and recordings, and provides lyrics to traditional Spanish songs suitable for babies as well as Spanish translations of age-appropriate songs in English. In addition to the Spanish-language version of the program, there is also an inclusive version that has been adapted for children with special needs, and a Hebrew version as well. For more information about any of the *Mother Goose on the Loose* programs, visit http://www.mgol.org.

## Choosing Stories for Storytime

Keep a few criteria in mind when choosing books to read aloud in preschool storytime. Make sure the story is short enough to hold the preschooler's attention. The vocabulary and syntax should be easy enough for children to understand. The story itself should be clear with characters and subjects that appeal to preschoolers. If the story has a plot, it should have a beginning, a middle, and a logical end. The illustrations should be large enough for the children to see, be colorful, and should complement the text. You should personally like the story, because your attitude will be reflected in the way your read it.

## Themes

Often preschool storytimes are built around a theme. Common themes are bedtime, farm animals, and teddy bears. Many professional books for librarians include examples of theme-based storytimes. These list books, fingerplays, activities, and sometimes even musical recordings with a common theme. Although there are many new books, some of the old classics are still valuable. A terrific resource is Carolyn Feller Bauer's series of books for librarians including: *This Way to Books, Leading Kids to Books through Magic, Leading Kids to Books through Puppets,* and *Leading*

Kids to Books through Crafts. Rob Reid's *Family Jukebox, Something Musical Happened at the Library: Adding Song and Dance to Children's Story Programs*, and *Shake and Shout* give ideas and suggest resources for adding music to programs.

Other sources that give great ideas for activities that go along with specific books are the *Story Stretcher* series (Raines, Miller, and Curry-Rood, Gryphon House) and *Mudluscious,* a book about food activities by Jan Irving and Robin Currie (Libraries Unlimited, 1986). The Internet also is a wonderful resource for programming ideas. In addition to blogs and sites for librarians, there are many sites for preschool teachers and child-care providers that list books, craft ideas, and rhymes. Some of these are "Shirley's Preschool Activities" at http://www. shirleys-preschool-activities.com/index.html, "Preschool Education" at http://www.preschooleducation.com, and "SurLaLune Storytime": at http://www.surlalunefairytales.com/storytime/index.html.

## An Example: Pajama Party (Bedtime)

Pajama Party storytime can be fun for the entire family. Choose books about bedtimes or beds. Many are funny ones such as *Llama, Llama, Red Pajama* by Anna Dewdney or visually exciting ones such as *Maisy Goes to Bed* by Lucy Cousins. Choose a few bedtime-themed songs that are easiest for everyone to sing along with, such as "There Were Ten in the Bed," or "Teddy Bear, Teddy Bear, Turn Around." Invite your audience to come in their pajamas and to bring their teddy bears with them. At the end of the program, serve hot cocoa. To give it a cozier feeling, you may want to wear bedroom slippers or have a big fluffy bathrobe wrapped around you.

Close with a lullaby. If you have visitors from other countries, ask them if they would feel comfortable singing a lullaby in their language.

## How to Conduct Theme-Based Programs

When planning a theme-based program, the librarian will first have to find a few picture books on the theme. Once the books have been chosen, it is time to look for a fingerplay or rhyme to go along with it. Rather than memorizing a rhyme you might never need again, one technique librarians have been using for years is to print out the text on a paper the size of an index card and tape it lightly to the back of the book that you will read just before reciting the fingerplay. Then, once you have finished reading the text, close the book, and hold up the cover for everyone to see. At the same time, you have a few seconds to look at the rhyme and refresh your memory.

## Structure

Many librarians adhere to the following structure for their preschool storytimes:

- Introduce yourself and welcome everyone

- Opening ritual

- Read longest book aloud

- Activity

- Read second book

- Stand up activity

- Read third book

- Activity

- Read fourth book—very short and interactive such as lift-the-flap or shout out the answer

- Recap

- Closing ritual

These steps are typical for a preschool storytime.

## Name Tags

You may want to have ready-made laminated name tags for young library visitors or to ask parents to make name tags weekly using labels and permanent markers. Although some children will rip their name tag off right away, it can be a useful tool for you. Children respond much quicker if you can call them directly by name. Parents enjoy hearing you address their child by using his or her name.

## What to Do with Outerwear

If a class is visiting the library in the wintertime and the students enter the story room with their coats on, ask them to take off their coats before starting and to use them as a pillow to sit on. When your program is over, it will be easy for them to find their own jackets. You may want to offer to help the teachers with getting the children ready. This may involve zipping up or buttoning jackets and tying shoes. Don't be surprised if children start coming over to you. If they see that you are helping, they will often prefer the novelty of the librarian helping them get ready rather than getting assistance from their own teachers.

## Atmosphere

At the beginning, even if you already know everyone at your program, it is important to start by introducing yourself and welcoming everyone warmly. Smile and say hello in an enthusiastic voice. The opening moments of your storytime create an atmosphere that will continue into the program.

As described earlier, ritual defines the space for a certain activity; rituals tell the program participants, "Now it's time to start," and "Now it's time to end." Best practices in preschool storytime are both to start and end with a ritual. This can be a song, a fingerplay, or a rhyme. When storytime was first offered in public libraries, the ritual consisted of lighting a candle at the beginning of storytime and blowing it out when storytime ended. Because of smoke alarms and safety issues, this ritual has been discontinued. However, children love rituals and a large number of librarians have both ritual opening and closing activities for their preschool storytimes. If you incorporate a ritual into your program and forget to use it one time, you will certainly hear loud protests from your young public. My favorite opening ritual is a fingerplay I learned from Claudia Homoki, a librarian in East Brunswick, New Jersey:

Alligator, alligator sitting on a log. (*Place the palms of your hands together; open and shut them to simulate a mouth opening and closing.*)

Down in the water he sees a frog. (*Place one hand over your eyes as if peering ahead.*)

Down goes the alligator. (*Hold one outstretched palm in front of you facing up, and the other outstretched hovering by your shoulder facing down. Swish the higher hand down, and slap the lower hand as it passes by.*)

Around goes the log. (*Roll hands.*)

Away swims the frog. (*Make a "swimming" motion.*)

You may want to repeat the rhyme a few times until everyone is able to recite it with you. To keep the children from getting bored, repeat it in several ways. For instance, after reciting it twice in a normal tone of voice, you might ask everyone to whisper it, then shout it, then say it very slowly, then quickly, in a deep voice, then in a high voice. The repetition becomes a fun game, and no one will say it is boring! Plus, because you have repeated the rhyme over and over again, by the final time you recite it, all of the children will be able to say the lyrics along with you.

After the opening ritual comes the meat of the program. Start by reading your first book aloud. At this time, children are the most attentive, so it makes sense to start with your longest book. Get a sense of who your audience is, and choose books of an appropriate length. Some 3 to 5 year olds might enjoy the story of *Corduroy,* an old classic by Don Freeman, but for others, it might still be too long. For some preschoolers, a book about a teddy bear might be "too babyish," and for others, it might be just right. Because of this, when you are planning your program, it always makes sense to have extra books on hand to suit children of different levels. Be flexible and willing to substitute at the last minute if need be.

Preschoolers who like a book may ask to hear it read over and over again. When you are about to begin a preschool storytime and a child pipes up, "I KNOW that book," you can use this enjoyment of repetition to your advantage. Simply say, "Isn't it a great book?" followed by, "Don't tell the other children what happens so they can find out for themselves," or "Now you have the lucky opportunity to hear it again!"

Reading book after book after book can get boring, and it is difficult for preschool children to sit still for extended periods of time. Inserting activities between the books is a good way to break the pattern. During these activities, the children have a chance to move and talk. The activity may involve fine motor skills or gross motor skills through fingerplays and creative dramatics. It might involve songs and rhymes. Perhaps a puppet will appear on the presenter's hand and ask the children questions such as, "Do you like chocolate ice cream? Everyone who likes chocolate ice cream please raise their hands!"

Follow each book reading or storytelling with an activity, such as a fingerplay or song. After two or three books, children often get restless, and that is a great time to ask everyone to stand up. Use an activity that requires movement, such as doing the "Hokey Pokey," singing "Head, Shoulders, Knees, and Toes," or jumping up and down like kangaroos. Once you ask the children to sit back down again, they should have the patience to sit through a few more stories being read aloud.

The stories that you read should be getting shorter and shorter. For a final story, you may want to choose something silly, very entertaining, or interactive. Lift-the-flap books that require your audience to shout out an answer are always winners. Alphabet books with one picture per letter are another way to involve children. You can say the name of the letter and its sound, and they can tell you what object is in the picture. If you use a counting book, point to each object and ask the children to count aloud with you.

When it is time to end storytime, hold up each book and remind the children of what they have read. Repeat any of the songs and fingerplays that you taught to reinforce it. Make sure to mention both the author and illustrator at all times.

Then, to end, use your closing ritual. Many people find that the opening ritual works well as a closing ritual also. For instance, I use "Alligator, Alligator" to both open and close a storytime.

## Asking Questions

When dealing with a large group and trying to maintain crowd control, it is helpful only to ask "yes" or "no" questions. Asking a question with an open-ended answer may result in one child telling a long-winded story that no one else is interested in. The story may go on and on and on, and the child may be almost impossible to stop. Rather than putting yourself in this awkward position, asking "yes" or "no" questions and having children raise their hands to give their answers is a great way to involve them while ensuring that the program moves along.

## Dialogic Reading

When you have a smaller group, you may want to ask questions of the children regarding the text. This is called "dialogic reading" and helps to develop many important early literacy skills. You can focus on vocabulary words, characters, plot, illustrations, sequences in the story, predictions, and summaries. Because dialogic reading is a great way to prepare children for school, children's librarians are encouraged to model it for parents, caregivers, and child-care providers. In addition to simply modeling dialogic reading, it helps to explain what you are doing and why it is important. For instance, "Children who enter school 'ready to read' have a much easier time than children who don't. Being ready to read does not mean being able to read already. But it does mean being familiar with language. It is connected with having a large vocabulary, understanding that the printed word represents spoken words, that words are composed of sounds." By giving the adults this explanation, you may be encouraging them to try dialogic reading at home with their child. Books such as *Peekaboo Bedtime* by Rachel Isadora (Putnam Juvenile, 2008) can be used as an "I Spy with My Little Eye" game and provide many opportunities for discussion.

In one-on-one situations, dialogic reading consists of an adult who is sharing a book with a child and encouraging the child to say something about the book, evaluating the child's response and then rephrasing it or perhaps adding information to it, and finally prompting the child to again say something that builds on the original comment.

Dialogic reading that encourages discussion about a book can work well in a situation in which the librarian is familiar with the group. If the librarian is less familiar with the group, it may not be as comfortable if it means cutting off a child who enjoys monopolizing conversations with extremely lengthy comments.

## Puppet Kisses Help with Transitions

If you expect difficulties in getting children to leave either the programming room or the library, have a puppet make an announcement just before the program ends, "Free Moose kisses, today only." Explain to the children that the Moose puppet would love to give each child a kiss, but he will wait by the door and will only give kisses as the children are exiting. Do not let your puppet kiss any child who seems shy or hesitant. Kiss the children on a place that seems as germ-free as possible. Face kisses are not a good idea when there are runny noses to consider!

If the same children come to your library programs on a regular basis, you may want to use one puppet as your program mascot. Bring him with you to every program, and always find a way to have him offer kisses to the children. They will become attached to the puppet, and knowing that he will be part of your programs will increase their expectations and enjoyment.

## Including Grandparents

Some libraries have programs that bring senior citizens together with young children. It could be a special grandparent storytime, or it could be a storytime that is brought to a local senior citizen residence. Seniors often enjoy interacting with young children and remember many songs from their own childhoods. Young children thrive on positive attention and often enjoy the attention of an elderly person. Thus, this type of program could be a win-win situation.

## Using a Flannel Board

Because preschoolers may not have the patience to sit through long stories, a flannel board provides a great way to help engage their attention. The typical library flannel board is an easel that has one side covered with felt. The Best-Rite 5-in-1 teacher's easel can be found in many library store catalogs or online. Because felt sticks on felt, storybook characters, flannel characters, fruits, and vegetables can all be represented by felt cutouts. Storytelling is made easier when you have a few flannel pieces that you put on the flannel board as you are talking. This helps you remember the sequence of the story and gives the children something visual on which to focus. When using poems or nursery rhymes, one visual representation for each rhyme is enough. It will serve as a reminder that you were planning on reciting that specific poem or rhyme and will give the children a visual representation of the activity.

You may also want to give flannel pieces to the children and ask them to come up to the flannel board at different times to put their piece on it. A cumulative story or one with specific sequencing would work well with this. A song, such as "Old MacDonald Had a Farm" that has a wide variety of farm animals also lends itself well to flannel board use. Give each child a different felt animal, or, if you have a large group, give one cow each to five children, one horse each to five children, one cat each to five children, and so on. When you get to that particular animal in the song, invite the children to come up and put their animals on the flannel board. Incorporating flannel board use in this way will address several learning styles at once: the visual when children see the pieces, the auditory when they hear the rhyme or story that goes along with the piece, and the kinesthetic when they actually walk up to the board and put the pieces on by themselves.

While there are books with templates for flannel board characters, you may also want to use the copy machine to make a color copy of a specific storybook character. Use tacky glue to stick felt onto the back of your color copy, and you will have a lovely piece to use.

Quite a few reference books for children's librarians include information about flannel board and templates for characters. A few notable books are *Flannelboard Stories for Infants and Toddlers* by Ann and Mary Carlson (ALA Editions, 2005), *Books in Bloom: Creative Patterns and Props That Bring Stories to Life* (ALA Editions, 2003), and *The Flannel Board Storytelling Book* by Judy Sierra (H.W. Wilson, 1997).

## Puppet Shows

Preschoolers love puppet shows. If a budget is adequate, hiring outside performers can be wonderful. If not, there are many books that give easy-to-follow scripts for puppet shows in public libraries based on folktales and children's stories. Some will be for one- and two-person shows. A children's librarian in a library with a large teenage population may want to work with the teenagers and teach them how to manipulate the puppets along with reading a script. Then the teens can entertain the preschoolers with a puppet show.

Finding ready-made puppet theaters can be difficult. Some are made of PVC pipes, but these can be hard to put together and keep together. Other theaters look beautiful but are hard to move. Patterns for homemade puppet theatres are available on the Internet and in books. It might be easiest to find handy volunteers in your community and ask if they will build a puppet theatre that fits your storage capabilities and your moving requirements.

When you are presenting a puppet show from behind a puppet stage and following a script that is more than three pages long, punch a hole at the top of each page. Insert a cup hook facing you on the inside of the puppet theatre. Reinforce the top of each script page with a piece of scotch tape and punch a hole in it or punch a hole and use self-stick reinforcements. Hang the script pages from the cup hook. As you finish one page, simply pull it off the cup hook, and the next page will be ready and waiting for you to use. If you have difficulty manipulating puppets while reading the script, try recording the script ahead of time. Then for the performance, you can move the puppets along to the recorded script without having to speak. This works especially well if you also want to add in sound effects or recorded music. You will still need to follow along with the written script to know what the puppets are supposed to say, so don't forget the cup hook!

Puppets are great to use in storytimes as well as for shows. If you seem to have a very shy crowd, you can introduce them to a puppet that is also shy. Every time you bring the puppet out to see the boys and girls, have him run back to hide under your armpit. After doing this three times, ask the puppet what is wrong. Have him whisper into your ear. Then explain to the children that the puppet is shy and will only talk if they say hello to him. It is amazing how well this works at getting children focused and attentive. Puppets can also ask questions like, "Raise your hands if you like ice cream." Puppets can introduce a theme, they can talk about how much they love coming to the library, and they can explain rules regarding behavior or boundaries. Using a puppet makes it easy to get a message across.

Because children respond well to puppets, they can also be used in a special type of animal activity. During storytime, you may want show the audience a canvas bag containing puppets or stuffed animals. Bring out the puppets one by one and ask the children to sing the name of the animal and the sound the animal makes. Preschoolers love to share their knowledge with others; being able to proclaim publicly the sounds of each animal can be an ego-building activity, and preschoolers take pride in their ability to rapidly produce the correct sounds.

## Scary Puppet Shows

Some puppet troupes present long and involved stories that can be either boring or frightening to young children. If you are going to present a puppet show, the rule of thumb is always be flexible. For instance, many preschoolers enjoy the dramatized version of "The Gunniwolf." However, what do you do if a child starts crying in the middle because he is afraid of the Wolf and his "Hunkerchas"? Feel free to alter the script. For instance, have the wolf step out of character, address the audience, and tell them that he is a very nice wolf, and he is very good friends with the girl's granny. He is just trying to teach the girl a lesson that she should not go alone into the forest, but he thinks he has scared her enough already. Then go back to the puppet show and have the wolf offer to show the girl the way back to her home if she promises in return never to ever, ever go into the woods by herself again.

# Performers

Certain kinds of performances almost always draw a good preschool audience. Puppet shows are often popular. Sports programs such as a basketball player who can spin a basketball on his finger, head, and knees for longs periods of time; rapid-fire jump ropers; and some fast dance programs attract attention of children of all ages. Storytellers may or may not command the attention of preschoolers. Singers and actors may be able to provide age-appropriate entertainment, but if they are aiming at an older audience, the content will be lost on a preschool audience. Be sure when booking performers to make it clear that they will be performing for an audience of preschoolers.

Find out ahead of time if performers will come with their own equipment or expect the library to supply a CD player, a sound system, or other items. Ask how much setup time is needed for the performance, and make sure the room is available well before the performance. Arrange when and where to meet the performer if he or she has never been to your library before. You may need to have water on hand (many performers prefer bottled water), arrange for parking if there are limited spots, or give directions if your library is hard to find. If performers need costume changes, make sure there is a private space that they can use. If they are bringing lots of equipment, be sure to arrange to meet them in the parking lot to help them bring their materials into the library.

Be sure to keep the performer's phone number in an easily accessible place; if the performer is not at the library 20 minutes before the performance is about to begin, you may want to call and find out if something has happened and the performance needs to be cancelled.

Before the performance starts, welcome your audience to the library, and introduce the performer. Do not leave the room unless absolutely necessary. The performer is there to perform, not to discipline. Unfortunately, parents or child-care providers may use the performance as an opportunity to drop off their children and browse for books in the adult section of the library. It is imperative that a member of the library staff be in the room with the performer at all times, ready to jump in when needed to allow the performance to continue seamlessly.

When the performance ends, thank the performer publicly, and also thank your audience. Wait until the entire room empties out, and then see if the performer needs any assistance in loading up gear and moving it back to the car. If possible, give the performer the check for payment on the spot. If not, tell the performer when payment can be expected. Write up a brief review of the performance and performer for yourself or to send to the person who books the performers. In addition to mentioning performance quality, include information about how easy it was to work with that particular performer. Details like whether phone calls and e-mails were returned in a timely fashion, whether the performer arrived on time, and whether the room was totally destroyed when the performance ended could have an effect on whether the performer will be invited back to the library. It will also help to jog your memory if another librarian calls for a reference.

## A Storytime Example

1.  Introduce yourself: "Hi my name is ____ and I am so glad to see you at the library."

2.  Opening ritual—recite "Alligator, Alligator"

3.  Read longest book aloud—*Alligator Baby* by Robert Munsch (Cartwheel, 2002).

4.  Activity—introduce alligator puppet. Recite:

    "Five little monkeys swinging in a tree.

    Teasing Mr. Alligator, "Can't catch me."

    Along came Mr. Alligator sneaky as could be … SNAP!

5.  Read second book—*Bark George* by Jules Feiffer (HarperCollins, 2000)

6.  Stand up activity—sing "Head, Shoulders, Knees, and Toes," going faster and faster until it is almost impossible to continue.

7.  Read third book—*Always in Trouble* by Corinne Demas (Scholastic, 2009)

8.  Activity—hand out bells to everyone. Ring the bells to the song "B-I-N-G-O." Collect the bells.

9.  Read fourth book such as *Where's Spot?* by Eric Hill (Penguin Group, 2003)—this is a very short and interactive activity in which children can shout out the answer as you lift the flap.

10.  Recap—hold up each book and ask the kids to vote on the book they liked best. Ask them to raise both hands, wave them around, and say "WOOO" if they liked everything that was done in storytime.

11.  Closing ritual—repeat "Alligator, Alligator." Announce that the alligator puppet is giving free kisses, today only.

# Bilingual Storytimes for English-Language Learners

Often, children who speak languages other than English will visit the library with their parents. They may be one dominant language in the community, or there may be a number of immigrants who all speak different languages. Older children may not speak English but may also not want to hear books on a low level when their emotional development is much higher than their language skills. Carefully choose books that have a high interest level but an easy vocabulary.

If you don't speak the language of the families attending your programs, see if you can find a volunteer in the community who would be willing to work with you. Teach that person how to read stories aloud, and together you can choose material before the program begins.

# Storytelling

Storytelling is a traditional part of children's librarianship. Instead of reading aloud from books, at one point librarians were urged to "tell" all of their stories. The storytelling tradition has been passed on, and many children's librarians continue to tell as well as to read stories aloud. Telling a story is more intimate that reading one aloud, because the teller often has direct eye contact with the audience. Without illustrations, the visual imaginations of children are awakened, and each child is able to perceive the story in his or her own way.

The best stories to tell to preschoolers are stories that they already know and can help with (such as "Cinderella" or "Goldilocks and the Three Bears"). Preschoolers also enjoy stories with repetitive phrases or words that they can call out. They like stories with predictable plotlines and happy endings.

Even if a story is a little old for the preschool audience, if the librarian is an experienced teller, projects her voice well, and looks directly at her audience while speaking, chances are that the preschool children will pay attention. Preschoolers respond best to storytelling if it includes direct participation by making sounds and imitating actions. Traditional tales such as "Stone Soup" can be used to invite each child to physically contribute an imaginary vegetable to an imaginary pot of soup. Props help to focus attention; storytelling combined with tell-and-draw or tell-and-cut stories are also a big hit.

A few guidelines for successful storytelling are the following:

- Only choose stories that you personally enjoy.

- Divide the story into sections with clues that can help you remember sequences. A list of a few written cue words can help keep the storyteller on track.

- Practice telling the story until you feel totally comfortable with it.

- Remember to breathe and pace yourself; don't speed up as you are telling the story.

- Maintain eye contact with your audience.

- Don't be afraid to use your own words, to be creative if you forget part of the story, or to alter the story if it is getting a negative reaction.

For more encouragement, Kendall Haven and MaryGay Ducy's *Crash Course in Storytelling* (Libraries Unlimited, 2006) covers many aspects of storytelling for the new librarian. Other resources are listed in the bibliography at the end of this book.

## Storytime Boxes for Teachers

Occasionally, libraries like to supply storytime materials in premade boxes that can circulate from teacher to teacher. One entire storytime is contained in each box, related to common preschool themes such as community helpers, seasons, and colors. In addition to books, these boxes may contain laminated song sheets with lyrics to rhymes, toys, games, CDs, and puppets. The multimedia approach enables child-care providers to supplement their own collections with a wide range of materials. Although it can be cumbersome to count all boxed items (including each individual puzzle piece) both before it is checked out and when it is returned, it is well worth the inconvenience to do so.

Some library systems provide variations on storytime boxes to lend out to parents with sick children. Disinfecting the items when they return is essential. Other librarians group materials by topic in a knapsack and allow these to circulate to all library visitors. The knapsacks may contain both board books as well as picture books, a CD and puppet, and a listing of other activities.

Some public library systems serving many libraries or even the state library use different boxes. Everything that is needed for a high-quality preschool storytime based on a theme is kept in a box, the boxes can be sent out to any library in a system, and the librarian has an entire program ready to go, without having to spend chunks of time planning a program or gathering materials. For more information about storytime boxes, see Kathy MacMillan's *A Box Full of Tales: Easy Ways to Share Library Resources through Story Boxes* (ALA Editions, 2008).

# Film Programs

Although children can watch a great deal of television at home, it is useful to show some excellent movies at the library. Weston Woods pioneered making short film clips based on children's picture books. Their name is still associated with high-quality audiovisual materials for children, although now there are many other companies that also make great videos and DVDs based on picture books. Animated films use cartoon-like characters, iconic films use close-ups and fade-outs of the actual book illustrations, and live action films use human and real animal actors.

Most screen times for short films are well under 30 minutes; it is easy to create a "film" program by showing a few of these. Displaying the books on which the films are based is an easy way to enrich the viewing experience. While the Weston Woods films generally reflect the contents of the book, some films may not exactly do this. In that case, you may want to read the book aloud and then ask your audience to pay attention as you show the film looking for similarities and differences. This challenge is often well received by children; it is a good way to ensure an attentive audience if you have a very wriggly crowd! Although there are always new books and films to use, some of the older ones are gems and should not be ignored. Two wonderful book and film combinations that stimulate great discussions by preschoolers are Don Freeman's *Corduroy* and Mercer Mayer's *A Boy, a Dog, and a Frog*.

Some feature-length films may also be of interest to preschoolers, although they seem to prefer the shorter selections. Before screening feature length films, check to be sure that your library owns public performance rights to them. Don't overlook fascinating nonfiction or documentary films while looking for material to screen.

# Craft Programs

The motor skills of a preschooler are not highly developed, so craft projects must be kept simple enough for them to be able to create the project without feeling frustrated. For instance, almost all preschoolers can color with crayons, but some can make very precise movements and others cannot. Not all preschoolers can use scissors effectively. When planning craft projects, keep this in mind.

Simple crafts can be combined with a storytime, or full craft programs can be centered around the reading of one particular book. Many craft books have great ideas for crafts and a wide variety of ideas can be found on the Internet as well. A Web site for paper toys and crafts related to holidays that is free for noncommercial use is http://www.thetoymaker.com/4HOLIDAY.html.

# Play-Based Programs

Programs such as "Family Place Libraries," which originated in Middle County Public Library in Centereach, New York, and has expanded to public libraries throughout the United States, provide a structure for a weekly program that involves play and toys. The librarian prepares a room with a wide variety of push toys, dolls, manipulatives, and puzzles. Adults are invited to bring their children for a session of free play. Librarians model play behavior with the children, and an invited professional from the community (dentist, speech therapist, nutritionist) plays with children and informally speaks with parents answering any questions that may arise. The program ends with a short circle time. Nutritious snacks and informational materials about community resources may be available.

## Using Programs to Promote School Readiness

Through programs, librarians can informally teach parents about school readiness and its importance. They can encourage parents to create a home environment that is set up to help their child succeed in school. This involves having a safe environment, daily routines, consistent nurturing between adult and child, verbal exchanges between adult and child, loving exposure to books, encouragement of curiosity and imagination, sharing of books in a loving way, and trips to the public library. A safe environment is one where dangerous substances, such as cleaning chemicals, are kept out of a young child's reach. Electrical outlets have plastic safety guards, and parents know not to leave a hot cup of coffee at the edge of a low table where a child can reach it.

Parents do not need to be wealthy to provide a print-rich environment for their children; making sure that there are always books from the public library around the house in view of the child is just as good as owning books. The main idea is that children see books as a natural part of their life and have warm, fuzzy feelings associated with them. Through developmental tips, parents will learn about the important role they can play in setting their children up for success. Through the activities, children will get a chance to practice the types of behavior that can affect their entire school career.

## Summary

By attending programs, parents learn myriad activities to use at home, in the car, while waiting in public places, and during toilet training. They learn different ways to share intimate time between parent and child. By listening to the brain tips mentioned by the library, they are given the satisfaction of knowing that by coming to library programs, they are exposing their children to new ideas and concepts, encouraging their brains to develop numerous new connections, helping their children develop multiple skills (social, musical, language, motor), and setting the framework for later success at school.

# CHAPTER 3

## Books

A major reason that families with young children visit the library is to borrow books. It is assumed that the library will have high-quality books and parents will not need to worry about finding something "unsuitable" on library shelves. Although this is not always the case, because borrowing privileges are free, the price is certainly right. But because there is not just one type of children's books, it is the librarian's responsibility to have a collection with the different types of books suitable for the different stages of a child's development. For instance, the youngest child does not have the fine motor skills to turn pages and may enjoy exploring the world by putting things in his mouth; therefore, cardboard books should be part of a collection for the youngest children. This chapter addresses the many types of books possible to stock in your children's room.

## Preschoolers and Books

Books have fun stories. They may have pictures of a child's favorite things. They may describe situations that are very familiar to the preschooler or tell the story of a character who is just like someone the preschooler knows. They may give facts about a topic of interest to the preschooler.

Connecting preschoolers with books can help them develop some early literacy skills. "Reading" a book by themselves helps them to experience page-turning behavior. By following along with the words, they can see that words are made of letters and that each word makes a specific sound. They will learn that some books help teach new facts about topics of interest to them. They can learn to look at illustrations, to recognize different styles of artists, and to see that illustrations are visual representations that help to explain or enhance the story. Most important is giving preschoolers the sense that books are fun, forging a connection between reading books with adults and positive emotions, imparting the knowledge that books may contain useful information, and creating an understanding that books are a normal part of everyday life.

Maintaining an adequate collection is therefore an important responsibility of the children's librarian. A wide variety of books for preschoolers should be available in the public library, and the children's librarian should be able to offer parents and caregivers some general tips about preschoolers and books.

Preschoolers who have been to storytime may like pretending to be the storytime lady. It is not unusual for children to sit in a chair at home surrounded by stuffed animals or dolls, and present a storytime. They may like to pretend that they are "reading" by holding the book, looking very carefully at the pages, and turning them one by one. They may simply enjoy holding the book while it is brought home and back to the library, as something that they are responsible for. This helps them learn the importance of books when they start school and throughout their lives.

# Board Books

Very young children do not read books, they chew on them! Being able to explore the book, taste it, and pull hard on the pages, is a natural part of the explorative nature of the young child. It is appropriate book-reading behavior for young children. That is why many libraries stock cardboard books. These books do not rip easily, their sturdy surfaces enable them to be wiped with a wash cloth, and they fit well into little hands. The cardboard pages are much easier for little fingers to turn than regular paper pages. Also, the illustrations are often colorful, and the text is minimal. Although board books work well with children from birth to age two, some preschoolers still enjoy using them.

## Indestructibles

A series of books for young children is called the "Indestructibles." These beautifully illustrated, wordless picture books are printed on a paper-like fabric that is used in safety suits and safety wrap. The illustrations in these books are vivid and brilliant, the pages feel like real paper, and yet it is almost impossible to tear any of the pages. The books are practically indestructible. They are designed for babies to grab, hold, and chew and can be cleaned off with a wet cloth. Parents whose children have difficulty treating books gently but who consider themselves "too old" for board books may find that Indestructibles are perfect for their children. The Indestructibles Web site (http://www. indestructiblesinc.com) includes educational information and early literacy tips. Ways in which the books can be used to encourage babies to talk and tell stories and descriptions of the way babies learn through chewing give plenty of good tips that librarians can share with parents of infants and toddlers.

## Books with Little or No Text

Wordless picture books are great agents for stimulating a child's imagination. Direct your parents and caregivers to share the book with their children, telling a story aloud that matches the illustrations as the pages are being turned. Caregivers may also want to ask their children (depending on the child's level of development) to tell them a story based on the scrutiny of the illustrations. Some older books work well with this; some favorite wordless books are Mercer Mayer's series "*A Boy, a Dog and a Frog*" (followed by a showing of the film or films), Molly Bang's *The Grey Lady and the Strawberry Snatcher*, and Noriko Ueno's *Elephant Buttons*. These books can also be used individually in a storytime program where children are invited to look at one page at a time and create a story for the storytime audience. In each case, children can become involved in the illustrations and will be able to tell you a simple story by following the progression from page to page.

## Nursery Rhymes

Although people tend to think of nursery rhymes only in connection with infants and toddlers, older preschoolers also enjoy them. Nursery rhymes are great for helping children learn how to read. They are fun to sound out because of their interesting language patterns and rhyming words. They often contain rich vocabulary words. Some nursery rhymes are gruesome or violent, and you may decide to change them slightly before reciting them aloud. For instance, in the traditional rhyme, the little old lady who lived in a shoe "whipped" all of her children soundly and sent them to bed hungry. Many children's librarians like the visual image of the woman living in a shoe with her many children but do not like the idea of her whipping her children. One simple word change from "whipped" to "kissed" or "hugged" alters the entire flavor of the rhyme, making it more palatable.

*Neighborhood Mother Goose* by Nina Crews contains popular, traditional nursery rhymes illustrated with photographs of multicultural children in urban settings. Preschoolers living in cities seem especially to enjoy this book.

In reaction to the traditional non–politically correct nursery rhymes, a new genre of books sometimes referred to as "Father Goose" has emerged. These include old rhymes that have been modified to sound politically correct or updated to reflect our modern world. For instance, in one version of "Rub-a-dub-dub, three men in a tub," one of the people in the tub is a video maker. To help choose from the many fine collections of traditional nursery rhymes, see the bibliography in Appendix A at the end of this book for specific recommendations.

## Big Books

Big books are oversized books that are often used by librarians or teachers in storytimes. Generally two feet by three feet, these are often larger versions of popular picture books and not solely published as big books. Useful for children with visual difficulties, these books can also help to keep the attention of children who are easily distracted. The pages can be hard to turn. Most big books are reserved for in-house storytime collections or for circulating teachers' collections only. A comprehensive list of big books is available at http://www.teacherbigbooks.com.

## Classic Picture Books

When preschoolers are ready for more than simple board books, the next step up is a picture book with limited text and simple pictures. A typical picture book has about 32 pages. Although there is text, the illustrations are an important part of the storytelling. Parents or caregivers can read the book aloud to the child but should be encouraged to ask the child easy questions that can elicit a verbal response.

Picture books can be also be lengthy and text-heavy on many pages. These are the books that require an adult reader. Although most preschoolers will not understand all of the vocabulary words, hearing them in context will give them a sense of what they are supposed to mean. Preschoolers may ask for a favorite book over and over again. Some classic picture books are *Caps for Sale* by Esphyr Slobodkina, *Freight Train* by Donald Crews, and *The Very Busy Spider* by Eric Carle.

# Concept Books

Children who are just beginning to discover the world are often attracted to concept books. Appealing to children from ages two to eight, these books usually focus on one of the following: letters, numbers, shapes, sizes, colors, and opposites. They range from small board books to large picture books. They may be wordless, have just one word per page, or use text to enhance the concept. Concept books can be interfiled on library shelves with other picture books or may be displayed in their own section for easy accessibility.

Prolific author and illustrator Tana Hoban (1917–2006) used photographs of everyday objects to illustrate concepts in books with little or no text such as "Count and See," "Circles, Triangles, and Squares," "More, Fewer, Less," and "Push, Pull, Empty, Full." Other authors associated with concept books are Eric Carle, Laura Numeroff, and Margaret Wise Brown. Lists of concept books can be found in individual online library catalogs as well as on Web sites for preschool educators, such as http://www.preschoolrainbow.org/book-themes.htm.

Parents who do not know how to read well or who cannot read English may find concept books easy to use with their children. They can simply talk about the pictures, ask their children to point or identify a certain picture, or, if their child is already speaking, have a dialogue about the illustrations. Although it is better for children to learn about concepts by actually experiencing them rather than by looking at them in a book, concept books provide a great stepping stone by encouraging language development and facilitating discussions between parents and their children.

# Participation Books

Participation books are books that invite children to call out answers, to recite phrases along with the librarian, or to perform specific actions. Lift-the-flap books, such as *Peek-a-Choo-Choo!* (Marie Torres Cimarusti, Dutton Juvenile, 2007), words with repetitive phrases such as *One Duck Stuck* (Phyllis Root, Candlewick, 2003), and *Alligator Baby* (Robert Munsch, Cartwheel, 2002), and books that invite children to call out the name of the illustrated object (*It Looked Like Spilt Milk,* Charles Shaw, Scholastic, 1988) all fit into this category.

# Easy Readers

Easy readers are books designed for children who are learning how to read. They use a limited vocabulary in short and simple sentences. They are often in chapter form. Fonts are generally larger than usual, and there is lots of white space, which makes it easier to read the limited text on each page. Accompanying illustrations are often simple and give hints that help beginning readers decode unfamiliar text. Also known as Beginning Readers or Early Readers, these books are especially good for children who are just learning how to read. These are usually a special size to make them easy for children to hold. Many of these are labeled as "step books" or "learning to read" and should be shelved in their own section of the library so parents can find them easily.

Transitional readers follow easy readers as a bridge to age-appropriate reading. Simple sentences, short chapters, and high-interest topics make these books popular among reluctant readers.

Some series are labeled in steps to help parents find books that are at just the right reading level for their children. In 1955, Theodor Geisel (more commonly referred to as Dr. Seuss) used rhyme, repetition, whimsical illustrations, and an incredible imagination to create the first easy reader, *The Cat in the Hat*. Still in print today, this set the stage for easy readers that were fun for children to read. Often humorous, these books are intended to inspire children to read on their own.

In 2004, the first Maryland Blue Crab Young Readers Award was given for the best fiction and nonfiction books that were both easy readers and transitional readers. Published for children from K to grade 2, for students from second to fourth grade, and for older readers with lower reading levels, many of the selections would also work well as read-alouds to preschoolers. Books that have been selected for this award include:

- The Fly Guy series by Tedd Arnold (Scholastic)

- *Bubble Trouble* by Stephen Krensky (Aladdin Paperbacks, 2004)

- *Ruby Bakes a Cake* by Susan Hill (HarperCollins, 2004)

- *Chicken Said, "Cluck!"* by Judyann Ackerman Grant ( HarperCollins, 2008)

- *Don't Worry, Bear* by Greg Foley (Viking Juvenile, 2008)

- *Giant Pandas* by Michelle Levine (nonfiction; Lerner Publications, 2006)

To obtain booklists of Blue Crab winners and honor books, visit http://www.mdlib.org/divisions/csd/blue.asp.

This local award was followed by the establishment of the annual Theodore Seuss Geisel Award, sponsored by the Association for Library Service to Children (ALSC). Beginning in 2006, authors and illustrators of the most distinguished beginning reader books written in English and published in the United States during the preceding year have received this award. More information about the Geisel Award can be found at http://www.ala.org/ala/mgrps/divs/alsc/awardsgrants/bookmedia/geiselaward/index.cfm.

# Nonfiction Books

Preschoolers are intrigued by specific topics. Cars, trucks, and trains may be a topic of interest for a four year old. Instead of simply relying on picture books, direct the child and his family to the nonfiction section of your library. Encourage them to explore nonfiction books with lovely photographs and clearly written information. Try incorporating nonfiction books into your regular preschool storytime.

# Audio Books

Audio Books, books on tape, or books on CD can be great for children. They often come along with a picture book, and a noise such as a "ding" will tell the children when to turn the pages. This is a great way to teach children book-reading behavior. Although it is preferable for parents to read aloud to their children to have the personal contact, once the parent has read the book, using audio books is a great way to help children develop vocabulary, to feel independent about their book reading, and to connect them with picture books in a more personal way. Some children have learned to read simply by following along with the text being read on CD. Others are able to enjoy longer stories with more complicated plotlines through listening to well-narrated versions.

# Fairy Tales and Folktales

Fairy tales can be gruesome, and in our politically correct world, many fairy tales are no longer read. Remember Little Red Riding Hood who went to visit her grandmother and was eaten up by the wolf? Well, there are more versions of that story; in some, the wolf was cut open by a woodsman and died. In others, he was cut open and lived; in others, he repented of his ways; and in yet another, he merely locked Little Red Riding Hood in a closet.

Bruno Bettelheim wrote about the value of fairy tales for helping children explore different situations and respond with different reactions. Preschoolers often like the scariness in stories such as Hansel and Gretel, in which their survival is in question, but in the end they triumph. Because most children in the United States are familiar with certain folktales, it could be useful to introduce them to icons such as the "Three Little Pigs" and "Goldilocks and the Three Bears." Familiarity with these classic tales will mean that the children will share a common book language with other children by the time they enter kindergarten.

Do not limit yourself to the traditional fairy tales by the Brothers Grimm or by Hans Christian Andersen. Include Anansi tales from Africa into your preschool storytimes. Regale your audience with tales about this clever spider who likes to play tricks on everyone. Some Anansi stories have been beautifully retold and illustrated by Eric A. Kimmel. His versions work well for storytelling as well as story reading.

Multicultural versions of some stories give children an introduction to other cultures. The story of Cinderella is told in many countries; *Cendrillion* is the Caribbean Cinderella in a beautifully illustrated version by Robert D. San Souci; *Yeh-Shen* is a Cinderella story from China that was written by Ai-Ling Louie and illustrated by Ed Young. A fun version that combines many cultures for older preschoolers who have good attention spans is *Glass Slipper, Gold Sandal: A Worldwide Cinderella* written by Paul Fleischman and illustrated by Julie Paschkis. Babette Cole has a funny mixed-up version of Cinderella about a prince with some mean and macho brothers called *Prince Cinders.* There are many more versions of this classic story!

## Fractured Fairy Tales

Some folktales have altered versions. For instance, the story of "The Frog Prince" has become *The Prog Frince* (Scholastic, 1999) and *The Frog Prince, Continued* (Puffin, 1994). Two very popular creators of fractured fairy tales today are Lane Smith and Jon Scieszka. With *The True Story of the Three Little Pigs* by A. Wolf (a story about the three pigs as told from the wolf's point of view) and *The Stinky Cheese Man and Other Fairy Stupid Tales,* the two men have hilariously used traditional tales to create funny spoofs that all children can enjoy.

To fully appreciate these versions of "fractured fairy tales," the children have to be familiar with the original first. For instance, if children hear the story of the Three Little Pigs in storytime one week, it might be fun to read aloud the story of the three pigs as told from the Wolf's point of view the next week.

## Books Related to Television Shows and Movies

Books for children are often made from television shows and movies. The quality of these books can vary. Many picture books are published by the Disney Corporation, and they will use their familiar cartoon characters as illustrations. Movies and television shows have also been created from books. These are generally popular, since it was the popularity of the book that inspired the creation of the television series. These include Arthur, the Berenstein Bears, and Curious George.

### Books by Celebrities

A relatively recent phenomenon is the introduction of books for everyone written by celebrities. Some of these work well, and others just seem to be cashing in on the fame of the writer. Read them yourself and decide which ones would be useful to own as part of your collection.

## Professional and Reference Books for Children's Librarians

In addition to books for children, there are a number of excellent professional and reference books for librarians. Patrick Jones, Rob Reid, Carolyn Feller Bauer, and Saroj Ghoting are all authors who have written professional texts that help in creating book-based programs for children. A bibliography of suggested books is included in Appendix B.

*A to Z* (Libraries Unlimited) is a reference book that catalogs children's picture books by subject. If a parent asks for books about sibling rivalry, a number of books can be found under that topic in *A to Z. Children's Catalog* (H.W. Wilson) and *Best Books for Children: Preschool through Grade 6* (Libraries Unlimited) offer brief descriptions of books which you might choose for your library.

Of course, with the advent of the Internet, it is also easy to look up book lists online. However, it is always useful to know about the print resources that can supplement the electronic information.

World Book has an excellent dictionary and encyclopedia that can be helpful to adults with curious preschoolers. Although many reference resources are available online, preschoolers enjoy finding an answer to a question or information about a topic of interest in an encyclopedia aimed at their age group. They may then thumb through the guide and find other entries that can capture their interest.

## Parenting Collections

As mentioned earlier, caregivers may want to improve their caregiving skills. Because it is difficult to take a young child into the adult section and spend time quietly browsing through bookshelves, many children's librarians have found it helpful to have books on parenting in the children's collection. With energetic young children in tow, it may be impossible for them to take time to peruse parenting books located in an adult section of the library. To help fulfill their information needs and provide a useful resource that will help with raising children, a shelf or area devoted to books for adults is the perfect solution. These books can deal with topics such as:

- Bedwetting

- Discipline

- Health

- Nutrition

- Songs and games

- Art activities

- Child development

- Dealing with crisis

- Children's friendships

- Sibling rivalry

## National Book Awards

Each year at the American Library Association meeting, usually held in June, selected children's books receive awards. The oldest and most prestigious of these awards are the Caldecott and the Newbery Medals.

Named after English illustrator Randolph Caldecott (1846–1886), the Caldecott Award is given to the illustrator who has created the most distinguished picture book in the United States during the preceding year. The illustrator must be an American citizen or a resident of the United States. The Newbery Medal was named for John Newbery, an eighteenth-century bookseller, and is awarded to the most distinguished contribution to children's literature that has been published in English in the United

States in the previous year. The author must be an American citizen or a resident of the United States.

In addition to awarding the medal to one winner for the Caldecott and one winner for the Newbery, honor books are also chosen. A large round sticker that looks just like a medal (gold for the winner, silver for the runners-up) is placed prominently on the cover of the winning books. These awards are coveted by authors, illustrators, and publishers; in addition to being prestigious in the literary world, they also guarantee enormous sales for the winning books. Although the majority of winners of both the Caldecott and the Newbery Medal are fiction books, nonfiction books occasionally win. The most recent nonfiction book to win the Caldecott Medal was *The Man Who Walked between the Towers* by Mordicai Gerstein (2004), and the most recent one to win the Newbery was *Lincoln: A Photobiography* by Russell Freedman (1989).

It is not unusal for an author or illustrator to win one of these prestigious awards more than once. For instance, David Wiesner has won three Caldecott Medals (for *Flotsam* in 2007, *The Three Pigs* in 2002, and *Tuesday* in 1992.) In addition, he won a Caldecott honor award for *Tuesday* in 1992. Jerry Pinkney won a Caldecott Award in 2010 for *The Lion and the Mouse* and in 2003 for *Noah's Ark*. He also won Caldecott honor awards for *The Ugly Ducking* in 2000, *John Henry* in 1995, *The Talking Eggs: A Folktale from the American South* in 1990, and *Mirandy and Brother Wind* in 1989. Sometimes, many years elapse between an illustrator's winning awards. For instance, Uri Shulevitz won his first Caldecott Medal in 1969 for *The Fool of the World and the Flying Ship*. His most recent award was a Caldecott Honor Award 40 years later for *How I Learned Geography* (2009).

It is interesting to note that although five of Laura Ingalls Wilder's books were named Newbery honor books, none ever won the Newbery Medal. On the other hand, authors E. L. Konigsburg, Joseph Krumgold, Lois Lowry, Katherine Paterson, and Elizabeth George Speare have each won Newbury Medals for more than one book. Kevin Henkes won awards for writing as well as illustration: *Kitten's First Full Moon* won the 2005 Caldecott Medal, and *Olive's Ocean* was a Newbery Honor book in 2004.

A committee composed of people who have been either appointed or elected is responsible for selecting the books. During the year, committee members read, read, read, and read. They make sure that the books they like meet the criteria and try to convince other committee members to choose their favorite. Committee members often state that the honor books are just as good as the winner; by the time it comes to select one book to be the winner, the choice has been whittled down to a group of books that the committee already considers to be the absolute best in their particular category that fit the qualifications for the award.

In the exhibit hall of the annual ALA Midwinter Conference held in January each year, publishers often use bright bookmarks to bring the public's attention to the books that they think are contenders for either of the awards. Librarians browse through the exhibits looking at books they may not have previously seen to have a head's up on all the books before the prize winners are announced at an early Monday morning press conference during Midwinter.

Similar to the Academy Awards, there is some controversy surrounding these awards. Occasionally, the Newbery award is given to a book that is well written but not particularly popular with young audiences. For instance, one year when the Newbery award was announced, there was a shocked silence in the ballroom; most of the librarians there had not ever heard of the book, let alone thought that it might be a Newbery winner. On the other hand, when a well-loved book wins, there are shouts, catcalls, standing ovations, and vigorous clapping.

At the ALA Annual Conference in the summer, a Newbery/ Caldecott banquet is held where the winners of the Newbery and Caldecott Award each give a speech. Children's librarians use this as an opportunity to dress in fancy clothing. Librarians from around the country attend this extravagant event to celebrate their love and appreciate of quality children's books.

Many library systems and schools run elections for a "Mock Newbery" and "Mock Caldecott" Award in November and December and post their findings on listservs for other librarians. These "preelection elections" make the press conference where the awards are announced even more exciting; with modern technology, many libraries now offer live broadcasts or Webcasts of the award announcements so that librarians who could not attend the conference or children who voted for books will be able to participate in the anticipation and emotional discovery of the winners.

Other national book awards chosen by committees and announced at the ALA Midwinter Press Conference are the following:

- The Robert F. Sibert Informational Book Medal for nonfiction

- The Coretta Scott King Book Award, which recognizes outstanding African American authors and illustrators who contribute to understanding and appreciation of all cultures

- The (Mildred L.) Batchelder Award for most outstanding book translated into English in the United States that was originally published in another language in a country other than the United States

- The (May Hill) Arbuthnot Honor Lecture Award, which chooses a critic, librarian, historian, or teacher of children's literature, of any country, to give a lecture in a chosen host site

- The (Pura) Belpré Medal to a Latino/Latina writer and illustrator who does an outstanding job of portraying and celebrating the Latino cultural experience in literature

- The (Andrew) Carnegie Medal for the most outstanding video for children released during the preceding year

- The (Theodor Seuss) Geisel Medal for an author or illustrator of a beginning reader book that has been published in the United States during the preceding year

- The Odyssey Award for Excellence in Audiobook Production

- The John Steptoe Award for new talent

- The (Laura Ingalls) Wilder Award, which goes to an author or illustrator whose books (published in the United States) have had a lasting impact

## Summary

The different types of books available for use in storytime were presented in this chapter. This information will be helpful for parents and caregivers who wish to choose books for their children. See Appendix C for a full list of all picture books mentioned in this and other chapters.

# CHAPTER 4

# Collections

Study after study has shown that exposure to books and rich language experiences in stimulating environments can make a positive difference in children's lives. More studies show that children living in poverty often don't own even one book, although we know that children do much better in school if they have grown up in a print-rich environment. Libraries can play an important role because they may be the sole source of books and programs for children.

Of course, there is only a limited amount of money to spend for book acquisition, and a limited amount of shelf space, and thus the librarian needs to choose materials wisely. This chapter provides help in evaluating and reviewing children's materials to make sure to purchase the best available.

## Evaluating and Reviewing Children's Materials

A valuable guide for evaluating and reviewing children's books is *From Cover to Cover* (HarperCollins, 2010). Author Kathleen Horning explains how children's books are published, about the different genres of children's books, and how to write reviews. This book is recommended reading for all children's librarians because it explains how to order and evaluate books for their collections. It contains a wealth of information that would be helpful for anyone recommending books for children, whether or not that person is responsible for ordering books for a public library's children's collection.

# Review Sources

Library journals, both in print and online, are a great resource for choosing materials for your library. They often provide reviews of books as well as multimedia materials and computer programs. Particularly highly recommended resources often receive starred reviews. These journals are described below.

The Children's Book Committee from the Bank Street College of Education reviews more than 6,000 books each year and publishes a list of the best 600 books (both fiction and nonfiction) for children each year. Book reviews are annotated and listed by age and category. An online copy of the list for children under age five can be found at http://www.bankstreet.edu/bookcom/best_under_five.html.

As mentioned as a reference book in Chapter Three, H.W. Wilson publishes its *Children's Catalog* that can serve as a guideline for maintaining collections of children's fiction, nonfiction, picture books, story collections, and magazines. This catalog contains descriptive annotations, excerpts of reviews from *Wilson's Book Review Digest,* and complete bibliographic data that can be useful when creating a core collection for a children's room. Available in electronic form, it can be searched in a variety of ways including reading level and topic.

*Booklist* has been the review journal for the American Library Association for more than 100 years. Delivering more than 8,000 *recommended-only* reviews for books, audio books, DVDs, and videos, it also contains information about popular genres and award winners and includes interviews with authors and illustrators. Now published in electronic form as well as in hard copy, *Booklist* has a forum for discussions, essays, columns, and quite a bit of useful information. The online version can be found at http://www.booklistonline.com.

*Book Links* is a quarterly supplement to *Booklist,* also published by the American Library Association, that provides annotated reviews of books, audio books, reference sources, video, and DVD titles connected to specific themes. Available online as well as in print, it also includes ideas for combining book use with activities, discussion questions, and information about authors and illustrators.

*School Library Journal* is a monthly publication published by Reed Business Information aimed at school librarians and media specialists. It provides reviews of books, multimedia materials, and reference resources. Highly recommended items are given starred reviews. The online version can be found at http://www.schoollibraryjournal.com.

*Horn Book (The Horn Book Magazine)* is a bimonthly journal that produces reviews and critiques of books and audio books, combined with essays and reports. Acceptance speeches by authors and illustrators who have won the Caldecott or

Newbery Awards are often reprinted here. Each year, *Horn Book* editors select and publish a list of best books. The *Horn Book Guide* is a sister companion that contains only reviews; well-indexed and produced semi-annually, it provides reviews for more than 2,000 books. The Horn Book Guide Online is a fully searchable electronic database of more than 70,000 reviews at http://www.hornbookguide.com/cgi-bin/hbonline.pl.

*Publisher's Weekly* is a trade publication that reviews books, audio books, videos, and materials in electronic formats before they actually become available to the public. The goal is to sell books, and the reviews may therefore not be as objective as those in the librarian-sponsored review resources. Over 7,000 book and media reviews are published in *Publisher's Weekly* each year.

## Regional Book Awards and Book Lists

Many states have their own book awards and recommended book lists. Capital Choices is a group of librarians, teachers, children's literature specialists, booksellers, and magazine editors in the Washington, D.C., area who meet on a regular basis to review recently published books and audio books. Yearly lists of outstanding titles for children and teens include books for young children up to the age of seven and can be found via the Capital Choices Web site at http://capitolchoices.communitypoint.org.

The Children's Round Table of the Texas Library Association publishes a yearly "2X2 Reading List" of recommended books for children from age two to grade two. These lists can be accessed online at http://www.txla.org/groups/crt/2X2intro.htm.

The Missouri Building Block Picture Book Award is voted on annually by preschool children in Missouri public libraries (http://molib.org/BuildingBlock.html). Every year, students in Maryland choose a picture book to receive the Black-Eyed Susan Award (http://www.maslmd.org/awards_winners.php), children in Connecticut vote on the Nutmeg Book Award (http://www.nutmegaward.org), children in New Hampshire choose a winner for the Ladybug Picture Book Award (http://www.nh.gov/nhsl/bookcenter/programs/ladybug.html), and children in Delaware vote on the Blue Hen Award (http://www.wilmlib.org/bluehen.html). School librarians and public librarians may suggest possible candidate books for the award and help facilitate balloting and voting.

If you would like to become involved in any of these state awards, contact information can be found by Googling "state book awards" or the name of the specific award for your state. Or, if you are looking for suggestions of books to add to your collection, you may want to browse through a number of these lists.

# Materials Other Than Books

Most collections in children's libraries now include materials other than books. Choices for these are described below.

## Magazines

Magazines include the monthly *Your Big Backyard* and bimonthly *Zootles*. Both feature beautiful photographs and information on animals for preschoolers. *Ladybug* has stories, games, poems, and songs for preschoolers, and its counterpart, *Babybug,* is a simpler magazine for children from babyhood until age 2. Also for infants and toddlers, *Zoobies* focuses on animals and is durable for little hands. It's lift-the-flap and peek-a-boo features invite interaction from children who are still too young to read (http://www.zoobooks.com/about_zoobies.aspx).

## CDs, Audio Cassettes, CD-ROMs, Videos, and DVDs

Preschoolers love listening to music; CDs and audio cassettes are a likely part of a public library children's collection. Children also enjoy watching DVDs or videos, so you may want to add some carefully selected items to your collection.

Because children love to listen to music, parents may rely on recorded music to put their children to bed at night, to keep them entertained while they are driving in the car, or to fill the time while they are toilet training. A good collection of CDs and audio cassettes can be helpful in these cases. Also, parents who want to sing to their children but who cannot remember lyrics to songs from their own childhoods may find these materials useful.

Some librarians circulate CD-ROMs with educational games for children. One type of CD-ROM reads books aloud and allows children to click on characters to see additional information. If chosen, the written text can be highlighted while the story is being read. More complicated CD-ROMs involve animated games, logic, and art.

Recent studies suggest that it is much better for young children to have live interactions with the adults in their lives than to be sitting in front of a television set. Although a program may be labeled as "educational," children may learn more by exploring and doing things themselves rather than passively sitting and watching something on a television or video screen. However, sometimes parents need a break, and a video or a DVD can provide just that. Having circulating videos and DVDs available in the library may be a wonderful resource for adult caregivers.

## Selecting Computer Software

When choosing computer programs, although parents may push for educational programs that focus on letter awareness, it may be more beneficial for their preschooler to choose software programs that encourage problem-solving skills, along with some letter recognition. Games on the computer can help children's social and cognitive development, language skills, critical thinking, and give them practice with decision making. Consider selecting software that fosters preschoolers' curiosity and comprehension of the world around them. Are the directions intuitive and easy to follow? Does the program run smoothly? Is the program physically appealing? Are there annoying noises, and is the sound level appropriate? Does the program encourage thoughtful planning or simple reflex action? If a skill is being learned, are there many opportunities for repeated practice? Since these programs are for circulation, be sure that they do not need the most up-to-date computer systems in order to run smoothly.

## Weeding a Preschool Collection

According to my colleague Melanie Hetrick, who is a weeder extraordinaire for children's books, there are a few principles to keep in mind when weeding your collection. She graciously shares her tips here.

The material found in a children's collection in a public library is often considered sacred. So when a librarian is told that the collection needs to be weeded, a large-scale panic attack may follow. This is to be expected. However, it must be done. To obtain and maintain a healthy collection, weeding is a must for all libraries.

If someone asked, "Why weed?" there are many reasons to offer for why a collection should be weeded on a regular basis. Most important to remember: books are not designed to last forever, and they don't. At some time in the life of all books, they begin to transmit communicable diseases. Also remember that children are very visually stimulated and can be easily overstimulated. Cluttered shelves full of ratty, old, and dusty books are not appealing to a child. Overstuffed shelves overwhelm kids, and unattractive books do not attract readers.

A useful acronym to help you while weeding is MUSTIE:

Moldy/Misleading

Unused/Ugly

Superseded

Trivial

Irrelevant

Elsewhere

*Moldy:* If a book is found to have mold in it, it should be discarded quickly. Mold can spread from book to book in a library and destroy entire collections. Two types of mold are most commonly found in libraries. One is the little white powdery dots found on the end pages of a book. It often looks like powdered sugar. The other is the standard greenish-blackish mold we often see in showers. Both kinds of mold can be toxic to anyone's health, and books harboring them should be discarded.

*Misleading:* If material contains incorrect or outdated information, it should be removed from the shelves and replaced. This also refers to materials that are missing for significant periods of time. Rather than leaving them in the library catalog hoping that they will eventually reappear, officially withdrawing them from the collection makes sense.

*Unused:* Materials that are not being used on a regular basis (at least two or three times a year) should be removed. In doing so, you will find space that can be filled with attractive new material, or simply keep your shelves from being cluttered.

*Ugly:* Materials that are dirty, torn, or stained or physically unattractive for other reasons should be removed or replaced if the item is important or popular.

*Superseded:* If there is new information available on a topic, old materials should be removed and replaced. This is especially true for the sciences.

*Trivial:* If your collection contains sufficient material on a subject matter, and there are books that really don't offer anything of additional value, discard them. Materials that lack literary value take up much-needed space in libraries.

*Irrelevant:* Material that does not fit within the needs of the community should be removed. For example, if your library serves children and you find an adult book, get rid of it.

*Elsewhere:* If the material is infrequently or never used and is available in another department or library, consider discarding the item.

## When to Keep Materials

There are several reasons for keeping material that is well used. If you are seriously attached to a book and you use this book in most storytimes, consider making the book a reference copy or taking it out of the library catalog and making it part of your personal collection. Look into ordering new copies because a favorite you use regularly will be sought after by the children to take home. It is important to keep material that is written or illustrated by local authors and artists.

Look carefully before you discard. Check publication dates on older books. Before discarding something that is really, really old, you may want to check to see if it is valuable.

## Diverse Families, Diverse Characters

Children like to hear stories and see pictures about children similar to them. Make sure that you have books featuring diverse families and diverse characters: children from multicultural families, children with single parents or same-sex parents, and children with immigrant parents who do not speak English, for example. These children all enjoy seeing someone like themselves represented in books. In addition, by deliberately including books about children who live with two parents of the same sex, just one parent, or with parents from different religions or racial backgrounds, you are painting a picture of the real world in your collection. Since the child's adult holds the library card, it is ultimately up to them whether they want to expose their child to lifestyles that differ from their own, but at least they are offered that choice.

In addition to providing books featuring diverse families, you may also want to have books with a range of diverse characters. In addition to cute bunnies and talking dinosaurs, you may want to feature books about children who live in homeless shelters, who come from other countries, or whose parents are going through a divorce. Some of the books dealing with children in particular situations can be preachy, and you may try to avoid these types of moralizing books. However, when dealing with situations such as the birth of a new baby (Keats, *Peter's Chair*), sibling rivalry, death (Partridge, *Big Cat Pepper*), a family member with autism (Lears, *Ian's Walk*) or a physical impairment, or joblessness (Hazen, *Tight Times*), picture books about a specific situation may ease the way for conversation and healing. The term for this is "bibliotherapy."

## Holiday Books

Children love to celebrate holidays, parents enjoy reading holiday books, and holidays make a great theme for display! Since most holidays occur just once a year, some librarians keep holiday books in their own section, or, if space does not allow, keep them off the public floor and only bring them out for display and circulation during the specific holiday time. Popular American holidays for preschoolers are Halloween, Thanksgiving, and Martin Luther King Day. Wintertime is associated with many multicultural holidays including Christmas, Hanukkah, Kwanza, and Eid ul-Fitr. Collections can reflect the religion and culture of your local community and can also introduce them to the cultures and traditions of other communities.

## Deposit Collections

A deposit collection is a significant number of books (perhaps 100) that has been specifically selected for a site. For instance, a child-care center might request a deposit collection of books to be kept there throughout the year. This book collection is checked out to the child-care center for long-term use, and no overdue notices are sent. At the end of the year, if not sooner, the books are returned to the public library, and they can be replaced with a new deposit collection of books.

Deposit collections for preschool sites generally consist solely of picture books. Teachers often request books with themes such as seasons, colors, community helpers and holiday books.

## Collection Maintenance

Occasionally, it is helpful to determine the state of an entire collection. If you hire pages or have helpful volunteers, they as well as librarians may be assigned to specific sections in the children's room (i.e., fiction, nonfiction, easy-to-read books). They will inspect each book individually and look for the state of the book's cover, if any pages are torn or mildewed, if the information inside the book is outdated, and if the book is still visually appealing. The goal is not necessarily to weed, but rather it is to check to see if there is enough material on topics of interest to children or if there are popular books that are looking worn and need to be replaced. Children should not feel responsible if a book in bad condition falls apart while they are looking at it. Also, if the book is in bad condition, they may not feel as obligated to take good care of it.

Shelf reading can also help to determine if there are enough books by popular authors and illustrators and on topics of interest. This may be a time to match books that are physically present in the library with books that are listed as being part of the collection. If books are missing, the librarian can determine whether to order replacement copies. Also, the librarian may use one of the "Best Books" lists to see if there are books that should be purchased for the collection.

# Summary

The key to an outstanding children's library is the quality and quantity of the books and other materials available to children and parents when they come to the programs being offered or when they simply come in to help their children select materials to take home. A major responsibility of the librarian is to ensure that parents and children find that quality and quantity when they arrive. If your collection is in need of additions and the budget is lacking, consider asking the community for help. Preschool children are an easy "sell."

# CHAPTER 5

# Reader's Advisory and Reference

Knowing the right book to recommend to a library patron, whether a child or adult, is called "Reader's Advisory." We all long to be able to match up the right book with the right child, but this is often not an easy task. To do this successfully, you need to know individual children's hobbies and interests. It helps to know what they have already read and their opinions about those books, what they liked and disliked, and why. Reading level or reading ability should also be taken into account; however, when children *really* want to read a book, reading level rarely deters them.

If adults ask you to help choose a good book for their child to read, it helps if you can speak directly with the child. Ask questions such as, "What is your favorite book?" and "Which authors do you like?" The adult may be able to help answer the question (most three to five year olds will not remember the name of their favorite authors), but it establishes the principle that you are looking to cater to the child's interests. Also, the parents may mistakenly think that their child's favorite is one book, where the child may believe a different book was better. Unless you include the child in asking the question, you may never discover that the child enjoys a particular genre of book.

Once you have an idea of the type of book the child might like, either take him or her to the appropriate area on the shelf (nonfiction subjects or picture book authors) or bring a few examples of the same type of book. Never content yourself with only offering one book. It is always best to provide a few options, so the child can feel comfortable rejecting some of them. If you only provide one book, the parent may think their child is being rude by not accepting your recommendation, and this can create tension between the parent and child.

The best way to know the right books for you to recommend is to READ, READ, READ! Know your collection! Even if you prefer longer fiction books, make sure to continuously browse through your picture book collection. Also, many nonfiction books are of great interest to preschoolers. These include books about dinosaurs, trucks, firefighters, and bugs. If you have older books in your collection, don't forget to look at them, too; older books are often ignored because their covers are not as exciting as the newer books, but on topics of interest to preschoolers, they can still be relevant and age-appropriate.

In addition, there are many resources with lists of recommended books for children. The Association for Library Service to Children (ALSC) publishes a number of book lists online that may be a useful resource (http://www.ala.org/ala/mgrps/divs/ alsc/compubs/booklists/index.cfm). Some public libraries also publish Web pages that include lists of suggested books for young children. Hennepin County Public Library provides a number of book lists for children from birth to age six at http://www.ala.org/ala/mgrps/divs/alsc/compubs/booklists/index.cfm. Also, the regional book lists mentioned in Chapter Four provide many timely and interesting titles for preschoolers.

## Criteria for Helping Others Choose Books for Children

Remind parents and caregivers that the best criteria for choosing books for their children is by reading level and by topic. Although most preschoolers will need to rely on an adult to read the book aloud to them, the topic has to be of interest to the child. A book with some unknown and difficult vocabulary words is fine; a book that is unintelligible because of all the big words used is not one that should be considered for a preschooler. One exception to the rule is if a child has a burning interest in a particular topic. For instance, when children are fascinated by dinosaurs, they may be able to learn terms such as "omnivore" and "carnivore" and are able to tell the difference and know the names of the different kinds of dinosaurs. A book written for older children on this topic that contains new information may be interesting to the preschooler, if the parent is willing to read aloud and translate when necessary.

## Book Lists and Bookmarks

Because parents often appreciate suggestions of good books to read to their children, a short book list with selected books or a bookmark that lists four or five titles may be exactly what they are looking for. These parents don't need the absolute best book; rather, they are looking for a high-quality book that they can feel good about reading to their child. Any simple solution you can give them to find these books will be helpful.

A few great books for preschoolers are the following:

Jane Yolen, *How Do Dinosaurs Say "I Love You"?* (Blue Sky Press, 2009)

Mo Willems, *Don't Let the Pigeon Drive the Bus* (Hyperion Press, 2003)

Bill Martin, *Brown Bear, Brown Bear, What Do You See?* (Henry Holt, 1996)

Esphyr Slobodkina, *Caps for Sale* (HarperFestival, 1996)

Robert Munsch, *Angela's Airplane* (Annick Press, 1988)

## Information and Referral: Answering Reference Questions

Before answering a reference question, you must first understand what the real question is. Adults often have difficulty phrasing their question to reflect the information that they need, and it is even more difficult for children to verbalize their information needs. Sometimes children filter out details. For instance, a boy may ask you for a book about horses when he is really looking for a picture book that has a horse as a main character. Before rushing off to the nonfiction section to pull multiple horse books off the shelf, take time to ask him a few more questions. These can include, "Are you thinking of any type of horse in particular? Do you know exactly which book you want? Can you tell me something about it?"

Children will often ask informational questions phrased in a way they think the librarian *wants* to hear. Rather than giving all the details necessary, they tailor the question to such a degree that the librarian may end up looking for the wrong information. The real question is needed for the librarian to provide a satisfactory answer. The best way to handle this is to have a short conversation with the child to draw out as many details as possible about the question itself or about details regarding the question. These few minutes of conversation may save tons of time and help avoid a wild goose chase; clarifying the actual question can point you in the right direction and help you look for the answer the child is truly seeking.

It can be intimidating for a child to ask an adult a question, so it is important to make the experience as comfortable as possible. Let children take their time in forming their question, and listen in an interested way. Feel free to ask questions for clarification, but be sure that the questions are asked in a respectful, interested fashion.

Don't overwhelm the child with an information request by bringing 25 books on the desired topic. Choose just a few books that you think are the best of the bunch and present those to the child. If it appears that they do not offer exactly what the child was looking for, then bring out more books.

## Summary

Although most librarians do not know every single book in their collection, they can provide great reader's advisory by having a sense of the popular authors and illustrators and the most well-used sections in the children's room. Knowing where to find booklists of best books, keeping on top of book reviews, and being able to smoothly navigate through their libraries' online catalog are skills that enable good customer service for reader's advisory and reference questions of preschoolers.

# CHAPTER 6

## Children's Room

Because a children's room is meant to be used by children, it makes sense that the physical design of the space should take this into account. Physical size of furniture, color scheme, and overall appeal should be geared for the intended audience. Libraries are not just focused on books but also include multimedia technologies, and so there will most likely need to be space for computers or gaming as well. Many libraries also have areas with toys. The key is to have a space that is welcoming to preschoolers but does not scream out "PLAYGROUND." The space should be designed in such a way that librarians are *not* forced to constantly remind children, "No running," "Please don't jump on the furniture," "That tree is for decoration and not for climbing."

Some libraries have a children's room that is on a separate floor or in a totally separate part of the library building. Other libraries simply have a children's area on the same floor as their adult collection, but the space is clearly marked and obviously meant for children.

The children's room is not supposed to be a quiet area where serious scholars concentrate on written texts. However, older children may use it as a study area. In addition, loud noise can be annoying and distracting to anyone. Therefore, although silence is not the goal, an atmosphere of soft and joyful communication with a sense of decorum is the idea.

In addition to keeping children in mind, since preschoolers will be visiting the library with a parent or caregiver, you must have adults' comfort in mind as well. You may want to create an environment where parents and caregivers are encouraged to have positive, physical contact with their children by offering reading nooks where adult and child can sit comfortably together to share books or guided activity stations where they are encouraged to play together. Early literacy stations with directed activities can help give parents some simple tools that encourage them to read, talk, sing, and play with their children.

## Essentials

Not all preschoolers are toilet trained, and so it is helpful to keep wipes on hand for parents to use in emergencies and to have at least one wastebasket for disposal of dirty diapers with a cover that can contain smells. A designated diaper changing area confines dirty diaper disposal to one trash can. A corner with a bit of privacy or a rocking chair will be helpful for a nursing mother.

Children who have just been toilet trained may be very proud of their ability to go to the toilet on their own, but a nearby toilet is essential. A child-sized toilet seat is most comfortable for preschoolers, but because the children are accompanied by their caregivers, having an adult-sized toilet would be greatly appreciated by many of the children's room visitors. If space allows, family-size bathrooms are the best, because a parent with a preschooler may also be accompanied by a baby and another young child. Drop-down changing tables attached to the restroom wall are also helpful, and, as noted earlier, wastebaskets with lids for diaper disposal are also appreciated.

Although the children's room seems like a safe place for children, there have been cases of children being bothered by adults near or in the children's room toilets. Thus, it would be ideal to have the entry to the bathrooms within vision range of the librarian sitting at the children's information desk. A sign stating that restrooms in the children's room are only for children and their caregivers, directing adults without children to the restrooms in the main area of the library, is essential.

## The Information Desk

Because the children's librarian may spend hours each month sitting at the information desk, it is important to make it a comfortable space. A telephone and computer should be within easy reach, and there should be a comfortable chair with adequate leg room. You will often be leaving your chair to help people on the floor, so there should be easy access in and out of the desk in a well-designed way that does not also invite the public to come behind the desk. Although preschoolers will not generally be doing school assignments, they may want to request a book on fairies or dinosaurs or some other topic of interest to them. For this reason, they must see the information desk as a welcoming place, and not an impenetrable fortress.

# Furniture

Because the children's room is a space specially geared for children, it is important to make it as welcoming as possible. Furniture that fits little children, including tables and chairs that are the right size for pint-sized library visitors, all give the message that "This is your room." At the same time, because young children do not come to the library without an adult, regular-sized chairs and tables are also necessary.

The ideal setting is one in which the librarian can sit at the information desk and see what is going on throughout the children's room. If your vision is obstructed, you may run into cases where parents get distracted talking to each other and unbeknownst to everyone, their children will use the time away from mommy's keen eye to pull all the books off a shelf. If there are no hidden areas, this can be avoided.

Many library companies supply safe and colorful library furniture. Soft, durable, and comfortable chairs, brightly colored book displays, and tables in all colors and sizes are among the offerings from these vendors. Alligator bookshelves, benches that look like the book spines, and mushroom stools are just a few of the colorful options available today. The intention is to create a space that sends a message to children, "This space is specifically for YOU," while also making it clear that the library is not a playground. Early childhood areas may include colorful carpets, soft climbing structures, and built-in educational activities.

A few traditional library vendors are Brodart (http://www. shopbrodart.com, see the "Early Childhood Section"), Demco (http://www.demco.com under "Furniture"), Highsmith (http://www.highsmith.com under "Library Furniture" and then under either "Children's Floor Furniture" or "Children's Reading Environments"), and Gaylord (http://www.gaylord.com under "Children's Supplies and Furniture"). Terrific wooden bookshelves and other unique high-quality furniture for young children can be found at Community Playthings (http://www.communityplaythings.com). However, there are many specialty companies that do wonderful things with library furniture for preschoolers. These companies often exhibit their wares in the exhibit hall during American Library Association and some state association conferences, and they also can be found online via their company Web sites.

Most library conferences produce conference booklets that provide program descriptions and schedules as well as listings of advertisers. Browsing through these booklets can provide names and contact information for many kinds of library vendors.

# Bookshelves

At least some of the bookshelves in a children's' room should be of a low height where children can reach all of the books. Some bookshelves have built-in mazes at the end, so children can use them as play areas. Freestanding bookshelves in the shape of animals have compartments that can easily store cardboard books, nursery rhyme collections, picture books, concept books, and easy readers. You may want to have a separate section for books on tape and audio books, although some librarians file them right on the bookshelf integrated in with the physical books.

Librarians can purchase shelving with wheels for the children's room. They can be easily moved to adjust the spaces for other uses. That is, you could create a storytelling area by pushing the shelving to the side and returning it as soon as your program is over. Make use of shelving with places on the end to display books and other resources as is often done in bookstores.

# Displaying and Arranging the Collection

Books packed tightly on a shelf do not attract children. They like to see the cover of the book, to determine whether they would like to read it. To give children the chance to see the book covers, it may be important to rearrange your library. Weed many of the books from the crowded shelves. Be merciless. Use the tips from Chapter Four. Then wisely choose the books to put back in your circulation collection.

Although the "bookstore" model may feel uncomfortable to you at first, once you see how quickly the books fly off the shelves, you will be inclined to display more and more books this way. Rather than packing the books into your shelves, make sure to keep the shelves no more than three-quarters full. Use a bookend to keep the books standing, and choose a book with a colorful cover to display to the public in the remaining space.

Books move more quickly if people can see what they are. The cover of a book is much more appealing than its spine. Stand books on top of shelves or use the bookstore approach of putting them on the ends of your shelves, cover on display. You can also leave them lying on the tables where children will see them. Some newer-design bookshelves keep picture books at preschool height and allow for displaying books by cover, rather than by spine. Gressco Ltd. offers animal bookshelves that are visually appealing and directed at the younger library visitors. You can find these and more at http:// www.gresscoltd.com/products by looking at both the Mar-Line and the Habba collections.

Generally, picture book collections are not kept in alphabetical order by the last name of the author. Rather, they are often only shelved by the first letter of the author's last name. The assumption is that little hands may come and pull multiple books off of the shelf at one time, and parents will want to be helpful by putting books back on the shelf. Although it may be harder for you to find books that are not in total alphabetic order, for the sake of the children and parents, it is much easier to relax these rules and simply alphabetize them using only the first letter of the last name.

As suggested earlier in mentioning audiobooks and their book counterparts sitting next to each other on the shelf, you may want to pull certain collections and shelve them together. Easy Readers and I Can Read books are one example. All the books by a particularly favorite author such as Dr. Seuss might stand alone.

# Toys in the Library

A few toys are often found in the children's section. Large wooden puzzles with pieces that are easy to manipulate, puppets and a puppet theatre, solid maze games, and blocks are common toys. Safety concerns must be taken into account when choosing toys; select nothing with small pieces that can be swallowed, nothing that might have lead paint, and nothing with sharp edges or parts that can inadvertently poke another child in the eye. Check federal legislation regarding toys with lead.

Another safety concern is health issues. Many libraries do not have plush toys because of the germs they collect. It is very difficult to clean them after each use.

Within the past few years, libraries have begun establishing early literacy corners filled with a variety of games that encourage early literacy skills. Matching games, letter recognition, experimentation with cause and effect, and exposure to shapes and different textures help children build skills that can help prepare them for kindergarten. These toys and games are best used when the children and their accompanying adult interact with them together.

Some librarians have found their early literacy areas to be so successful that they have expanded them into separate rooms or even entire sections of the library. "Little

Heights" in Ohio is a room set aside for free play, and "Storyville" in Baltimore County offers a children's museum experience by providing several themed areas designed beautifully for learning through play.

Another way in which librarians can provide high-quality play experiences for children is by circulating toys. To do this successfully, the librarians have to make a commitment to clean and disinfect the toy each time it is returned. Circulating big items with just one piece is much easier than circulating puzzles or games which rely on a number of pieces. Yet the inconvenience to the librarian may be far less than the benefit to the child who will be able to develop skills by playing with a toy at his or her own pace, at home. Individual toys can be kept in a sturdy plastic bag, knapsack, or tote bag and may include one or two books that have some type of connection with the toy.

# Computers

Pursuant to the passage of the Library Services and Technology Act (LSTA), earmarking telecommunications discounts for libraries and schools, the federal government created discounted E-rates for public libraries to help make technology more accessible to the public. In response, almost all children's rooms in public libraries began offering computers with preprogrammed educational games and online card catalogs. Computers just for children were placed in children's rooms. Because children seemed to like playing on the computer together, some computer stations were designed with social interaction in mind. Benches, rather than individual chairs, accommodate parents and children who need to sit together or siblings who want to play together on the computer.

Today, it would be unusual to find a children's room without a computer. Most have the preprogrammed educational games; some also have Internet access. Part of the children's librarian's job is rebooting the computer, explaining to parents and children how to play certain games, and asking children to lower their voices when they get too enthusiatic about their computer play.

A list of great Web sites for kids hosted by the Association for Library Service to Children and the American Library Association can be found at: http://www. ala.org/gwstemplate.cfm?section=greatwebsites&template=/cfapps/gws/default.cfm. These include a fair number of sites for preschoolers as well as sites for older children.

Although the library may have computers with Internet access, these are not ideal for preschoolers. Although there are sites with fun and educational age-appropriate games for them, it often takes more than "one click" to find them. Also, preschoolers are not known for patience or delicate handling. While waiting for a computer to reboot, it is not unusual to see an impatient preschooler begin pounding on the keyboard or clicking the mouse over and over, trying to bring on an immediate response. The response their actions may bring, however, is to freeze the computer yet again or to ruin the keyboard.

Although computer stations with preprogrammed educational games may be networked and connected to the Internet, the children are usually limited to playing the games displayed. Popular games often include recognizable characters such as Elmo, Bob the Builder, Thomas the Tank Engine, or Dora the Explorer and cover a wide range of subjects including English, math, and science. Programs may include matching games, art and drawing activities, puzzles, finding hidden objects, "reading books" by clicking on an arrow to turn pages, recognizing shapes and colors, typing exercises, and navigating through mazes. Programs may be available in languages other than English.

Many librarians use The Early Literacy Station AWE for their very young visitors (http://www.awe-net.com) because it is easier than having to choose and purchase a selection of games and their licenses for loading onto computers. In addition, these self-contained stations are educationally and developmentally age-appropriate; they are visually appealing and easy for young children to navigate. The physical equipment is robust and has been designed for use by little hands. Each computer comes preprogrammed with age-appropriate games and has been designed to ensure reliability. A starter package for children from ages two to five is filled with games about English, math, science, music, and art. Touch screens make navigation easy for small fingers, and librarians appreciate computers that do not need to be consistently rebooted.

# Exhibits

If a children's room is big enough, there are traveling exhibits that can be rented or borrowed. These liven up the atmosphere and teach in a fun way. For instance, Literacise provides an exhibit that is a kid-sized, bilingual children's book. There are tunnels, doorways, and secrets to find that enable children to experience the book from the inside. In addition, the exhibit comes with information panels for parents and educators on the importance of physical exercise to learning. The exhibit can be rented from www.literacise.com or (617) 266-0262.

NASA has traveling exhibits, as do many children's museums. Publishers sometimes create large cardboard figures or scenes to advertise upcoming movie tie-ins with books. Librarians on a budget can also find exhibit material from local merchants by simply asking if they can have the exhibit for a particular sale item once the season has passed.

## Summary

An inviting children's room with the right-sized furniture for young visitors, materials that appeal to children of all ages, seating for adults, and a welcoming librarian set the scene for an appealing place for families. Exhibiting books in an attractive way helps children easily make choices.

# CHAPTER 7

# Policies, Procedures, and Managing the Children's Room

Written policies protect children's librarians from irate adults and help to keep children safe. A few policies are essential. Most cover safety issues. The first has to do with adults who want to visit the children's room without a child.

## Unattended Adults

Unattended adults are adults without any accompanying children in the children's room, and they pose a big problem. Librarians have experienced incidents of adults flashing young children or bothering them in other ways. To protect the children and shield them from inappropriate activity, a policy regarding adults without children in the children's room is essential.

Children's librarians may not be aware of the sex offenders or pedophiles in the community, but common sense says that unless an adult comes to the children's area accompanied by a child, they should have a good reason for being there. Students of children's literature, art students looking at illustrations, child-care providers looking for books to take to their centers, or adults with developmental delays who can only read books on an easy-reading level are the types of adults who have reason to be in the children's room without a child. It is important to find out *why* the adult is there, and even if the explanation is plausible, keep an eye on the adult to make sure this person is really doing what was stated as the reason for being there.

When unattended adults come into the child's section, ask why they are there. If the adults say they are students of children's literature, ask them for the name of the course and institution where they are taking the course. You may find book illustrators who are looking for other examples of illustration, preschool teachers preparing lessons plans, and family members preparing for visits from very young relatives. Occasionally adults with reading disabilities or developmental delays come to the children's department to look for nonfiction and fiction with larger print and simpler vocabulary. For example, adults who need a very easy explanation of a topic such as magnets or electricity may want a nonfiction book to help them understand the basics, and these might be in the children's non-fiction collection.

However, for safety's sake, it is helpful to approach any adults who enter the children's area without a child and ask how you might be able to help them. If they do not have a purpose that sounds reasonable, you may want to ask them to leave or contact someone else on the library staff who is in a position to ask that person to leave and escort them out of your space. Or you may choose to ask another librarian to come into the children's section to help you keep an eye on things. When it doubt, it is important to trust your instincts. While always remaining polite to library visitors, it is vital to make safety for children a top priority.

## Unattended Children

Parents often think the library is a safe place for their children. Parents with young children may feel isolated at home and welcome the opportunity to chat with other adults when they are together at the library. This may mean that they do not pay attention to their preschoolers, assuming that they will be fine. However, children can slip out of the children's room undetected, they can clog toilets with paper towels, they can knock over book displays, bang on computer keyboards, rip jackets off of books, climb in the most unlikely places, or even slip out the door onto the street.

Although we want parents to feel that the library is a fun place for them as well as for their children, it is important for them to know that the librarian is not a babysitter. In some libraries, written policies posted by computer stations state that children under age six must be accompanied and supervised by adults while using the computers.

Occasionally an adult will ask the librarian to look after her child for just a few minutes while she runs to another part of the library to check out a book. Although most librarians would love to oblige and help out, there are many issues to be considered. What if the parent leaves, and the child has a temper tantrum? The child might start suddenly missing mommy, and mommy may not return for twenty minutes. That means that for twenty unending minutes, you may have a screaming child in the middle of your children's department. Of course, all libraries are different, and you may live in a community where that type of looking after another's child for a few seconds is acceptable. But good sense says that it should be avoided.

Other issues may arise with unattended children. A child may be highly allergic to peanuts and may inadvertently touch a peanut butter sandwich that may have fallen out of another child's knapsack. The child's parent would recognize the symptoms of an allergic reaction and know what to do, but the librarian might not have a clue.

Federal law states that children under a certain age cannot be left in public places without an adult. Occasionally, a very young child will be put under the custody of an older sibling who is not particularly mature, and the parents disappear. The children may get hungry, and there is no food, or a child might need toileting help, and the older child is unwilling to help. The librarian is then forced to become involved. All librarians should become familiar with their own state laws about unaccompanied children, because the age may vary from state to state.

## Behavior in the Children's Room

Young children do not always understand what good behavior is. Parents and caregivers don't always reinforce good behavior. Some parents or caregivers think that children must be absolutely quiet in the library, and this is not true. Conversation in a normal tone of voice is perfectly acceptable.

The ideal is for parents and children to go to the bookshelves together. Parents may show some books to their children on a particular topic, and their children will pick out books of interest to them. This is more empowering than simply having the child sit in a chair while the parent picks out all of the books. On the other side of the issue, we do not want a parent who sits down in a chair and watches (or does not watch) while their unsupervised child pulls book after book off the shelf and then walks away leaving a pile of material that needs to be reshelved in their wake.

Children who are not familiar with books may think it is fine to rip out a page with a nice illustration or use a crayon to scribble in a book. If you see this happening, it is fine to gently tell the child about "library behavior." If you see a child who has just eaten a messy sandwich and neglected to wash his hands, you may want to remind him that many people wash their hands before looking at a book to make sure that bits of their jelly sandwich don't end up on the pages of the picture book. Saying this in a friendly, non-judgmental way while pointing out the closest location for sinks may be a way to save your library books as well as your good relations with the child and his family.

When children misbehave, the librarian sometimes feels placed in an awkward position. Generally, the parent or caregiver is responsible for the child's discipline. When the parent or caregiver is ignoring the child, the librarian must do something. Some adults may consider that as taxpayers, it is their right to expect the librarian to be their child's teacher or, worse yet, babysitter. Then they may complain bitterly to the librarians' supervisor if they are not happy with the way their child was reprimanded. Policies help parents understand library behavior that is expected of all children, including theirs.

Always speak gently but firmly. One solution is to have a list of library manners available, maybe on a bookmark, that includes talking in a normal voice, treating books respectfully, walking rather than running, getting along with other children in the library, taking turns on the computers, sharing toys, among other policies. If a child begins acting out, you may want to tell her all about library manners. If things do not change, you may want to tell her and her caregiver that to remain in the children's room, they need to be using their library manners. If the child misbehaves one more time, you may ask them to leave, but to come back the next day with their library manners.

If a child has a temper tantrum and starts screaming in the middle of the children's room, many librarians feel awkward asking the caregiver and child to leave. One way to handle this situation is to suggest in a friendly manner that the child might have an easier time calming down if taken to a quieter place. You may ask caregivers if they would like to use a programming room, or to take the child outside for a few minutes, in the hope of giving them an easier place to focus and calm down. Be careful to do this in a diplomatic way so the caregiver does not feel that you are kicking them out of the children's room. Show that your concern is for the child rather than for your own eardrums.

## Library Cards, Overdues, and Renewals

To take books out of the library, a library card is needed. When I was a little girl, it was a *big deal* to finally be able to write my name so I could sign the card myself. I felt such pride when I received my first library card after signing on the dotted line. For preschoolers, this is no longer the case. Parents can get library cards in the names of infants who cannot yet speak, let alone write their name. This may cause problems relating to overdues, lost books, and renewals.

Some librarians worry about how to cover the legality of charging for lost materials if the child is a minor. It could be easier if parents take out children's materials on the parent's card and thus will be the responsible party. This is not without problems, however. When preschoolers really love a book, they want to hear it over and over and over again. Mom might be tired of the book and ready to exchange it for a different one at the library. But Johnny may ask for the same book repeatedly. If this is the case, how can mommy return the book? She may be able to renew it online, but this doesn't always work, especially if the children are intent on keeping the book for many months.

Rules concerning the length of time materials may be checked out from the library are meant to keep the circulation of items in order, but with the unpredictability of young children, sometimes flexibility makes more sense. A child may *love* a certain book. The parent reads it to their child every night at bedtime and hopes to return the book by its due date. The child does not want to give up the beloved book. The family may have already renewed the book three times and know that the library policy clearly states that a book can be renewed no more than three times. They should try to renew it anyway! Encourage them to call the library and explain that their preschooler has fallen in love with the book and would like to read it again. If no one else is waiting to borrow that particular book and if they have called before the due date, they may be allowed to keep the book out a little bit longer.

Recently, other librarians have come up with another solution for this. Some libraries have created cards especially for children under the ages of five or six. At the Enoch Pratt Free Library in Baltimore, this card is called "First Card." The card is actually taken out by adults on behalf of their children. Only children's materials may be borrowed on the card. However, in recognition that young children love to hear the same story repeatedly and that parents are often sleep deprived and unable to adhere to strict schedules, there are no overdue fines associated with timely return of material. If a book is returned even six months late, all is well, and no questions are asked.

Some libraries provide "teachers' cards." Day-care providers may have to show proof that they work in a center, but with such a teacher's card, they are given special privileges such as being able to check out multiple copies of the same book or taking out many books on the same subject. For example, if a preschool is covering a unit on seasons, the teacher may ask to take out a number of books on the same topic. Some libraries do not allow more than a certain number of books on a topic to circulate, but teachers are exempt from this. Again, teachers do not pay overdue fines, allowing them to keep the books until they have finished a unit without having to worry about constantly renewing them.

# Computer Policies

Preschoolers should be spending the bulk of their time actively exploring the world around them by seeing, hearing, feeling, tasting, listening, and doing. Experiencing the world via a computer screen does not have the same value. Yet the computer holds fascination for children, and some parents are very anxious for their preschoolers to become computer literate. Some wonderful games are available for preschoolers to play that encourage math skills, logic, and deduction. Some games help children develop fast reflexes. Other programs read aloud to children while highlighting each word as it is read; some art-based programs allow children to create their own masterpieces. Children get experience following directions by listening to the instructions of a narrator to play a game. Although it is easy to get a child interested in playing games on the computer, it can be difficult to get the child off of the computer.

With limited computers and a stream of young visitors, it is important to set up policies regarding computer usage that guarantees time for everyone. Although there are some systems that automatically time out after 30 minutes, sparing the librarian from having to police computer use, a visible written policy that limits computer time to somewhere between 30 minutes and an hour is standard. Having this backup protects the librarian against protests by both children and their accompanying adults.

Many libraries have policies that require children under a certain age (including preschoolers) to be accompanied by an adult while they are on the computer. This can help keep the computer to remain in working condition. The assumption is that an adult will prevent the child from smashing on computer keys, crashing a mouse repeatedly against a desktop, or putting slobbery fingers all over the computer screen. Also, if an adult is with the child, the adult will hopefully be able to answer questions about when and where to click and how to play the games. Without an accompanying adult, it is not unusual for the children's librarian on duty to hear a never-ending succession of requests for help.

Sometimes, adults bring children to the children's room, get them set up on one computer, and then move to another computer to check their e-mail or do their own work. Some librarians are fine with this. Others with limited resources feel it is important to limit computer use to children. Although many libraries filter the sites children can access, this is not universal. Should an adult access inappropriate material while using a computer in the children's room and a child sees this, it would create an unpleasant situation. Again, a posted policy helps to avoid misunderstandings and bitter feelings regarding computer usage.

## Filtering and the Children's Internet Protection Act

The Children's Internet Protection Act (CIPA) is a federal law that imposes filtering on computers in school and public libraries in return for receiving a discounted E-rate from the federal government for Internet access. These filters block child pornography as well as content that is considered obscene or harmful to minors. Libraries that receive the E-rate must accept the filtering, although it can be disabled when requested or needed.

# The Children's Librarian as a Manager

The children's department is often considered an independent area within the library. A children's librarian is not simply a librarian for children; the job involves policy management and supervision as well. Leadership, people skills, and managerial skills are expected of the children's librarian. The librarian deals with children, caregivers, adult visitors, other librarians, pages, and community partners. The librarian must be aware of library policies and ensure the smooth functioning of the children's department while keeping good humor and the sense of flexibility that is essential when dealing with children. Instead of being isolated, it is the librarians' responsibility to keep lines of communication open with other library staff, reminding them that children's librarians do much more than sing "The Eency Weency Spider." In addition to being familiar with children's literature and programming and knowing how to deal with children, the librarian must also be well versed in the technical skills necessary for running a library department.

## Monthly Reports

Many library trustees like to see usage statistics, and the library director may require submission of monthly reports. These may include number of programs presented and attendance figures broken down by age, that is, infants, toddlers, preschoolers, adults, and family programs. You may be asked to list type of programs (crafts, films, book-based). You may want to name day-care centers visited and home day-care groups that have visited the library.

Rather than looking at monthly report writing as an imposition, it can use used as an opportunity to brag. Describing all of the successful programs held during the month may help your library director realize the value of library services to children. Keeping track of figures for reference questions asked, computers used, and program attendance can also help when comparing the current year in the library with previous years.

The monthly report can be used as a vehicle to record anecdotes and stories that parents have told you. Funny anecdotes combined with hard figures may be recounted in library newsletters or used as illustrations to donors regarding the impact the library makes on the lives of community residents. Anything positive is worth jotting down; you never know when it might come in handy!

## Supervising Pages and Volunteers

In many large and medium-sized public libraries, the children's librarian is not obligated to put books back on the bookshelves. Generally, this is a job reserved for "pages," and in smaller libraries, volunteers may do this. Although larger libraries may have one person or department that is responsible for training and supervision of all pages, medium-sized libraries and branch libraries often delegate responsibility for pages to the various departments in which they are working. Smaller libraries will be responsible for this training. In any case, it would be the children's librarian's responsibility to train the page or volunteer how to put books and materials in the correct place (following the Dewey Decimal or Library of Congress System or, with picture books, by the first initial of the author's last name). Here are a few tips:

- Make sure the pages always sign in and sign out so that you have a clear idea of times in which they are supposed to be working.

- Familiarize your page with the cataloging system used by your library (Dewey or Library of Congress). Give a quiz on paper asking for a list of pretend items to be put in order. If you would like help with creating a quick quiz, search online or in literature teaching library skills.

- Give the pages a cart of books to shelve. Ask them to pull out the book slightly to the left of the one being shelved, put it in a horizontal position, and keep it sticking out slightly on the shelf. When the page has finished, look at the books to make sure they have been put in the right place.

## Summary

To keep the children's department running smoothly, the children's librarian must be aware of the policies of the entire library as well as those specific to the children's room. This can affect the safety of the children visiting the library, the well-being of the collection, and the functioning of the staff. Clearly articulated policies serve to protect librarians from ambiguous situations and benefit both family visitors and library staff.

The children's librarian must also be aware of management skills needed to manage the department. This includes supervising pages and volunteers who work in the children's room.

# CHAPTER 8

## Partnerships

This chapter covers finding partnerships in your community to expand your programming to the preschool child. It also covers advertising these events so that you will reach your intended audience and encourage their participation in your events. Finally, class visits to the library and visits by the children's librarian to day-care centers and schools are described.

No matter where you live, you can enrich your services to children through partnerships. If you are in a very small neighborhood or town, you might partner with a children's librarian in another library to present puppet shows and skits to both of your audiences. By sharing, volunteers for special events in one location might be willing to repeat the performance in another library.

Some of the services you might like to offer, such as programs with a visiting author or performer, have a price tag attached, and you may have a limited budget. Opportunities to share the funding needed for such programming with one or more libraries or with a school district or a nearby bookstore means everyone wins. It's only a matter of finding those partners.

Here are more suggestions for partnering with your local community helpers, which is an important focus of study. Inviting others in the community to visit the library during your storytime is always a public relations event.

# Potential Partners

## Police Departments

Invite local police officers to come to the library and read a book or two aloud to the children. This allows them to see police officers in a helping capacity. If the department has a canine unit, read *Officer Buckle and Gloria* and ask the local police to join you for the storytime with one of their dogs. There are often routines that the dogs perform that can be very entertaining for preschool children. If your area is under the jurisdiction of the state police, you might ask to have someone from that unit visit your library.

## Fire Departments

Nothing is more appealing to many small children than a big red fire engine with the firefighter in uniform. If you are in a rural area with a volunteer fire team, a member of this group can also be an effective speaker, showing children how they are being protected. If a child has a parent who is a volunteer on the fire team, he or she may be able to talk about the radio contact in their home.

## Health-Related Programs

A visit from a doctor or dentist who is willing to come to speak to children can be combined with stories about children going on their first visit to the doctor or dentist's office. Depending on the partner, the program may include giving away free toothbrushes or providing referral information for parents. Because many young children think they would like to be a nurse when they grow up, someone in a nurse's uniform who can talk about working in a doctor's office or a hospital can also be helpful.

Interview someone from the local health department about keeping children safe and turn it into a podcast or webcast that can be downloaded by anyone from your library's Web site. This can be helpful for the parents or caregivers that you serve.

## Barber Shops and Beauty Salons

For some children, going to the barber or beauty shop for a haircut is a very stressful situation. Invite a local beautician to talk about haircutting and perhaps demonstrate putting on a cape and listening to the sound of scissors. If possible, ask your visitor to give a puppet a haircut. Make sure to prep your partner ahead of time, noting that he or she will be speaking for only five minutes or so. Ask the hair stylist to talk about things he or she thinks will be interesting for the children. Follow this talk with books about hair, going to the barbershop, or visiting a beauty shop.

Encourage your hair stylist to speak with moms who are in their salons about bringing their babies and toddlers to programs at the public library. Ask if you can leave flyers about upcoming events there. Often, clients have time to wait in a hair salon and are looking for something to read. This is a great place to advertise events!

## Beauty Schools

If beauty schools have sample heads with hair that they will donate to the library, these can be used for a program called "Rapunzel's Hair Salon." From a beauty supply store, buy mannequin head holders and attach them to the top shelf of a book truck. Put the heads on them. Display different book versions of Rapunzel on the middle shelf. On the top shelf, in a basket or box, keep brushes combs, and colorful hair clips. Invite children to help style Rapunzel's hair. If possible, get heads with all kinds of hair such as blond, Afros, spiky hair, and long hair. This is a great way to let children experience other textures and colors in a safe way.

## Restaurants

Invite the chef or owner of a local restaurant to participate in a program. You may want to read a story about food and then ask your visitor to talk for a very short time about his or her profession. Include creative dramatics by making an imaginary dish following a recipe. If you have the facilities, perhaps the chef would like to give a cooking class with a simple recipe for toddlers. This is good advertisement for the restaurant and is fun for the children.

## Pet Store Owners, Veterinarians, Dog Breeders, or Horse Owners

Most children are fascinated by animals, and there is a wide variety of professionals and laypeople who can be approached about presenting programs. A pet-store owner, a local veterinarian, or a member of a group such as International Therapy Animals might be willing to present a program about pet care. A parent or volunteer who shows horses could bring in a saddle and speak about a horse's different paces. Through creative movement, children can learn the difference between "trot," "canter," and "gallop."

## Other Local Merchants

Invite other local merchants to present a preschool storytime with you. Choose books on the theme and ask the merchants to speak very briefly about what they do. For instance, read some stories about gardening and flowers and invite the local florist to talk about working in a flower shop. If the florist brings a few different types of flowers to the preschool storytime, the children can be guided to notice the various smells, colors, sizes, and shapes of the flowers.

Your community will have others who could come to the library: airline pilots, flight attendants, a bookstore employee, the first-grade teacher, and the school crossing guard or school bus driver. By simply looking around and noticing all those who help in your community, you should be able to find people who your children would enjoy meeting.

## Local Schools

Art departments have students who can provide help decorating the children's room or making flannel board characters for you. Some teens need community service hours to graduate high school, and this is a great way for them to use their talents to help benefit children's programming.

Music departments of high schools and colleges can present concerts or provide live background music for special events. A brief introduction to a particular musical instrument, a performance of one short song, and then an invitation to touch the instruments or try to play it (with supervision, of course!) is an enriching and fascinating program for preschoolers.

If the local schools have a drama department, call one of the teachers and ask whether there are a few students who would be willing to try out their performance skills by presenting a short show that is age-appropriate for a preschool audience. If there is a teacher who is looking for a project, try suggesting a dramatic performance of a popular picture book story.

## Community Groups

Karate clubs: Instructors of karate clubs or other child-friendly martial arts clubs can be asked to give child-powered demonstrations as entertainment for a library event; children who take karate lessons may be encouraged to give a demonstration for a library talent show.

Museums, science centers, aquariums, and zoos: for those libraries in a reasonable proximity, these agencies often can bring programs to the library. Preschoolers love petting live animals and doing art projects that involve unusual materials. They are fascinated by science experiments that produce different colored liquids or make noise. In return for providing the library with programs, the children's librarian can visit each of these institutions and offer storytimes based on their themes. For instance, a storytime in the museum might be based on the museum's collection of drums, and a storytime in an aquarium might include stories about fish and sea creatures.

4H clubs or The National FFA Organization (Future Farmers of America): Members of these clubs are often willing to bring live animals to the library. Create a display of picture books that include stories about those particular animals. Children can pet animals such as rabbits and learn about caring for that pet. If you are in an urban setting but have enough room, you might want to bring farm animals, such as sheep, to the library. While you may need to get permission from the Health Department first (which could include filling out forms and displaying a certificate at the site), this provides a wonderful opportunity for urban children to pet and learn about animals.

## Universities and Colleges

Astronomy departments: If there is a nearby college or university, librarians can tell folktales about the moon and the stars, then have a graduate student describe telescope use and invite everyone to come to the university on a specific night to look through the university's telescope.

Neurology clubs: Each year, there is "Brain Awareness Week" in March. Students in the clubs may be interested in coming to the library and running programs for children that include doing brain-building activities or fun activities that simulate the functions of the brain. It is important to work with the students ahead of time and not expect them to simply come to the library and present a program. They may have great ideas, but you need to make sure that they are choosing age-appropriate activities and that the program flows well.

Cultural clubs: Students studying a foreign language may belong to a cultural club that celebrates all aspects of culture from a particular country. These students may enjoy dressing in regional costumes, teaching a few words in a different language, and describing or acting out unusual customs. The librarian can read or tell a folktale from that country.

Education departments: Some undergraduate education degree programs require students to do fieldwork. Invite students to plan and present a program for a special event at the library. Be sure to contact their teacher ahead of time to ensure that the students get credit for their work and to have quality control over the program that they plan to deliver.

### Local Nature Centers

Local nature centers or state or local parks may have programs on bugs or reptiles that children will find fascinating. Families may be unaware of their existence, so by inviting representatives from these centers to the library, you are providing families with another age- appropriate destination. Encouraging exploration and appreciation of the outdoors may translate into more physical activity for families, which can lead to healthier lives.

## Class Visits to the Library and Librarian Visits to Schools

Class visits happen when day-care center teachers bring their children to visit the public library as a class; "school visits" describe when a librarian leaves the library building and goes to visit the day-care center. When the library is within walking distance of a day-care center or if transportation is available, day-care classes may come to visit the library. This is a great opportunity to give a tour of the children's room, pointing out the different materials, picture books, audio books, nonfiction, board books, and easy readers that are available, as well as other activities, such as computer games, building blocks, and a scribble corner. When showing young children the nonfiction section, it is worthwhile to point out areas that may be of interest to them, such as, "Here is where you can find books on dinosaurs, on animals, on space."

Point out areas with games or toys and briefly mention the library rules regarding that area. It is important to let children know that they are expected to put the blocks away when they are done *before* they start building a four-foot-high tower. If you have a drawing area with crayons, you may need to remind children that crayons stay on the table and do not move around the library.

Be sure to point out the bathrooms and show the children where the information desk is. It might be useful to have someone role-play a reference interview to give children the clear idea of how to ask questions. Whenever possible, introduce other librarians. If you have more than one person, staff member, or volunteer in the children's section of your library, be sure to introduce this person. It is always good to introduce the library director as the person who is in charge of the library. Make sure that the library is a welcoming space for all your visitors, and encourage them to come back to visit with their families.

This may be a good time to speak about library manners. Although libraries are not the stereotypical quiet places that they were once perceived to be, they are still public areas with people who are trying to work, play, and communicate. Therefore, children should be reminded that it is not a playground, and loud voices, screaming, and running are not acceptable library behaviors.

Bring library card applications to day-care facilities after they have scheduled a library visit but before it takes place. Ask the administrators there to have each child's family fill out an application and bring it into the library before the visit. Or ask if one of the teachers can collect the family signatures and then drop off the completed applications to the library a few days before the actual visit. By doing this, when the class comes to the library, there will be a library card waiting for each child. The children can end their visit by selecting books and checking them out at the circulation desk.

When visiting preschools for a "school visit," it is useful to bring a canvas bag full of books. Make sure you have a number of items suited to different levels. Although you may expect to be doing a storytime for thirty 5 year olds, you may end up with a class of 1½ to 2½ year olds. So bring books that are very simple with bold pictures and little text, and also bring some substantial picture books with complicated plotlines in case you get a sophisticated kindergarten class.

Always come with at least one song and fingerplay. "If You're Happy and You Know It" or "The Wheels on the Bus" are the two songs that almost all children know and are very easy for others to pick up once you start singing them. Use these songs to introduce yourself and as fillers in between books just to add variety.

A bag of colored scarves is always a useful tool. The light weight makes it easy to transport, and the scarves help children become involved in activities. Children can use their imagination to make the scarves into animals, clothing, or objects depending on the stories being read. Preschoolers take great delight in scrunching up their colored scarves into a ball, counting to three, and throwing them up in the air, then watching all the colors come drifting down. This simple activity can be repeated a number of times, and the fascination does not diminish.

Try to present your program in the typical "circle time" area; the children will already be used to sitting in that particular place and paying attention to the adult up front. Keep your props behind you or on a shelf near you if you are presenting to children who might try to come up and take the props away as you are presenting the rest of the program. Let the child-care providers know that you expect them to be part of the storytime. This is not a time for them to take a break to do their lesson planning! You do not know the students at all, and it is unsafe for a teacher to leave the children alone with you. Also, if you are in the middle of a program, you don't want to have to deal with a child trying to climb on your lap, a child pretending to sleep and snore loudly, two children hitting each other, or children who try stuffing the scarves into their mouths. You want to be able to continue smoothly with your program and not have to worry about taking time to oversee discipline.

Caregivers who participate in the program will also become familiar with the fingerplays and stories being read. They will then be able to repeat these after the librarian has left and integrate it into their curriculum. The program becomes a shared experience between the teacher and the class; in addition to helping to expand the teacher's repertoire, there is the bond-strengthening result of a shared experience.

## Special Events

Occasionally, you may want to hold special events at your library that require more staff members than you have. Community partners provide the perfect solution. For instance, for Children's Book Week or National Library Week, you may want to have extra activities in the library. Set up some folding tables, and ask art students from the local college to run a bookmark-making activity. Or ask the education department of a local cultural institution to bring some type of activity that someone from the institution can run on a drop-by basis throughout the day at the library. It will be good publicity for them, and it will provide an unusual and exciting activity for you. Inventors' clubs, and weavers' guilds can showcase their creations while providing related, age-appropriate activities for preschoolers.

In return for having a museum run a "table" for you, you may offer to present a storytelling program for them. Go the museum ahead of time, look at the artwork, and choose a few paintings that have some relation to stories you like to tell. One day when the museum is open for free to the public, give a family storytelling tour. Walk with your group around the museum, stop in front of the selected pieces of artwork, and tell the related stories. It is a great way to publicize the library to a crowd of people who might not be library users.

## The Institute of Museum and Library Services

The Institute of Museum and Library Services (IMLS) is a government agency that provides grants to support both libraries and museums. Some of these grants specifically encourage partnerships, with a strong emphasis on Library-Museum collaboration. A visit to the IMLS Website (http://www.imls.gov) gives a list of the various types of grants that are available; a database allows users to search all awarded grants by category. This is a good source for learning about partnerships that have already taken place and can give great ideas for replication.

# Summary

Partnerships are a great way to expand your programming with limited resources and may present a way for your library to reach as many people as possible. On a small scale, it can save money by helping organizations or individuals pool resources. On a larger level, it may require extra funding but can greatly improve and expand the library services offered.

Through partnering, you can inform new people about the services the library has to offer and also help to publicize whatever your partner has to offer. Be sure that the type of program you are planning will be beneficial to your partner as well as to the library and that it fits into both parties' goals. Be clear about what the partnership entails, and write down the expectations of both partners. Be sure to have contact information for everyone. For more information on partnerships, see *Children's Services: Partnerships for Success* (Diamant-Cohen, ALA Editions, 2010).

# CHAPTER 9

## Working with Special Populations

The public library serves everyone, regardless of race, religion, culture, sexual orientation, or economic background. Children also come in many different shapes and sizes. They may come from wealthy homes, welfare homes, or homeless shelters; they may have different abilities or disabilities; they may have one parent, two parents, stepparents, divorced parents, and incarcerated parents; their families may speak only English, some English, or no English at all. The information needs and level of early literacy skills in each child may vary greatly. Thus, it helps to look at the different populations using the children's room to be aware of the different types of services that might be useful.

## Children with Special Needs

The term "special needs" can address different children's conditions including autism, attention-deficit/hyperactivity disorder (ADHD), Asperger syndrome, bipolar disorder, Down's syndrome, obsessive-compulsive disorder, Tourette's syndrome, visual impairment, hearing loss, physical challenges, learning disabilities, as well as being gifted and talented. Children who fit into these categories may behave differently than other children because of their biological differences or because of their different learning styles.

Librarians working with these children see that flexibility is a must because the children's behavior can often be unpredictable. In addition to being warm and welcoming, it is helpful if the librarian also presents a calm and reassuring demeanor. Behavior rules that children without special needs have no difficulty adhering to may have to be adapted for those with special needs. Noise levels and movement restrictions during programs may change. However, one rule must stay consistent: no child is allowed to hurt others.

Some libraries hold programs specifically for children with special needs. For instance, the Matthews Branch of the Public Library of Charlotte and Mecklenberg County in North Carolina offers monthly family storytimes for children with autism, Down's syndrome, and other special needs. Online resources and videos about conducting a special needs storytime can be found on their Web site: http://www. plcmc.org/ programs/Special_Needs/default.asp.

When presenting programs, a few adaptations are helpful:

- Speak slower. Try to enunciate your words clearly.

- Describe, especially for visually impaired children, what you would like them to do. For instance, instead of simply saying, "Put your hands like this," give a step-by-step description, such as "Close your hands into two tight fists. Spring them open with all of the fingers spread out as far as they can be from each other."

- Find tactile representations for songs or stories. For instance, give each child a piece of wool or furry material to hold while a story about a sheep is being told.

- Repeat songs, rhymes, or instructions more often than is typically done.

- Consider having soft music playing in the background.

- Make sure any crafts you are including in your programs are doable for your audience. Because the process is more important than the product, it does not make sense to have a craft that the adult will do for the child.

- Rely on picture cards or storyboard software to let children know what to expect. A storyboard uses digital software to create standardized visual representations that facilitate communication with a child or help a nonverbal child communicate with you.

- Choose musical instruments that do not make loud noises that auditorily sensitive children will find upsetting.

# Children on the Autism Spectrum

Children on the autism spectrum may not be capable of keeping quiet or still. This can be disconcerting to library visitors as well as librarians. Autism is the fastest-growing developmental disability, yet many librarians are not sure how to handle children with this disorder.

"Stories on the Spectrum" for children between the ages of three and eight who have developmental disorders on the autistic spectrum have been offered at the Darien Library in Darien, Connecticut. The Multnomah County Library in Portland, Oregon, provides monthly Sensory Storytime for preschool children on the autism spectrum. Designed specifically for children who have difficulty keeping still during storytime, research and partnering with local organizations has helped them design unique programs. Librarians use storyboard software to create signs that define activities, and parents are encouraged to participate fully.

In New Jersey, the Scotch Plains Public Library and the Fanwood Memorial Library joined forces with other partners and produced a customer service training video for library staff to help them learn about autism and give them tools to serve individuals with autism and their families effectively. Information about the video can be found at: http://www.thejointlibrary.org/autism.

# Working with Deaf or Hard-of-Hearing Children

Children love sign language. Even if a child is not yet speaking and whether or not there is someone in the family who is deaf or hearing impaired, very young children find it easier to first communicate via signing rather than through speech. Kimberley Taylor-Dileva's *Once upon a Sign: Using American Sign Language to Engage, Entertain, and Teach All Children* explains in detail how babies can use sign language before they can speak, and she offers illustrations for children's librarians to learn and use sign language in their programming.

Children who have not been exposed to sign are fascinated when watching an interpreter "speak" through hand motions and facial expressions. It is therefore easy to include sign language into your programs for preschoolers, and everyone will benefit. Kathy MacMillan is an experienced children's librarian who is also an expert in American Sign Language. Her book, *Try Your Hand at This: Easy Ways to Incorporate Sign Language into Your Programs* (Scarecrow Press, 2006) is a wonderful resource with many suggestions for using sign in early literacy programs.

## Children with Delayed Speech

In British Columbia, children's librarian Tess Prendergast and a community partner who is a speech therapist present storytimes for children with language delays. These programs involve more repetition than is found in a typical early literacy program, and words are clearly enunciated. Everything moves at a slower pace than the usual program and children are given many opportunities to interact verbally. The involvement of the speech therapist has been instrumental in the success of this program. For more information on this, see *Children's Services: Partnerships for Success* (Diamant-Cohen, editor, ALA Editions, 2010).

## Children with Visual Impairment

According to a federal mandate, each state must have a special library for the blind and physically handicapped. These libraries are wonderful resources. In the past, they provided devices such as cassette players or CD players and mailed books on tape or CDs to people. Although advances in technology have occasionally resulted in switching old machines for new types of listening devices, the provision of "Books on Tape" (books that can be listened to) remains an essential part of these libraries' mission. Such services are not just for the visually impaired but can also be used by people with any type of disability such dyslexia and ADHD or for anyone who has, even temporarily, been incapacitated.

These libraries often have books in Braille for sighted preschoolers with visually impaired parents. In some cases, the books look like picture books, but there is a transparent sheet of plastic in front of each illustrated page. The adult can show the book illustrations to their children while "reading" the Braille aloud. Storytimes offered by a blind adult for sighted and visually impaired children can make use of these books. Seedlings Braille Books for Children (http://www.seedlings. org/about.php) provides a wide range of popular picture books at reasonable prices to libraries by purchasing the print books and then sticking clear plastic strips with Braille letters over the printed words.

If your library does not have many Braille resources, you should call your State Library and ask the children's librarian about services for blind or physically handicapped children in your community. Forging a relationship with this area of the State Library can be useful during the Summer Reading Club; special materials may be provided by the State Library for these children.

# Children with Physical Challenges

Children born with physical impairments or who acquired them as a result of accidents or illnesses face numerous challenges. Babies with low muscle tone may have had trouble turning their heads; this causes a delay in being able to see instantaneously what they hear and can result in an inability to focus, difficulty paying attention, and struggles to concentrate. Thus, the physical challenge also becomes a social one. Be patient with these children and create opportunities for them to interact in a positive way with others during your programs.

Limited arm movements or lack of fingers can hinder participation in craft activities. Confinement to a wheelchair may mean the inability to dance and perform some creative movement activities. Plan accordingly! If you have children who are physically challenged attending your programs, be sure to plan an activity that everyone can do or be prepared with a modified version that will suit their skills.

Recommend books on tape for children with visual impairments.

Remember that children confined to wheelchairs need a comfortable space that has plenty of room for maneuvering and an accessible bathroom in or close to the children's area.

# English-Language Learners

Because immigrants from around the world continue to settle in the United States, many communities have groups of English-language learners (ELL). A town that might have only had English speakers just ten years ago might now have a sizable population of Spanish or Hmong speakers. Even if the librarians do not speak the native language of the ELLs in their community, they can do a number of things to make these families feel comfortable in the library and willing to bring their children to programs.

- Print basic library information in the languages used in the community. Have available translated copies of library card applications and policies.

- Post translations of important signs in the languages used by the community. Signs for libraries in Spanish can be found at the Web site: http://www.tsl.state.tx.us/ld/projects/bilingualsign/ index.html.

- Identify anyone on the library staff who speaks the language used by new community members. This can be done with special name tags identifying themselves as a speaker of that language.

- Learn at least one song or rhyme in the language of your ELL community to use in your programs. You may want to ask one of the parents to teach a simple song in that language to everyone during a storytime program and repeat it in the following weeks. By encouraging library visitors to share their heritage with you and other library visitors, your program is enriched, the new visitors feel welcome, and an atmosphere of mutual respect between people from different cultures is created.

- Purchase books in the language of your ELL community whenever possible. Be sure to display them in an area where your library visitors are sure to notice them.

Parents who want their children to learn English may think that the best way to teach them is *not* to speak their native language at home. Their mistaken hypothesis is that children who are exposed to English on television and in their neighborhood will learn English quicker if they are not confused by also hearing words in the language of their parents. This is not true, however. Studies clearly show that children who have large vocabularies in *any* language have an easier time in school. It does not matter if the parent speaks in English or another language. The most important gift they can give to their children to prepare them for school is to sing to them, talk to them, and read to them in any language. An additional benefit is that these bilingual children may then be able to speak two languages fluently, a skill found in many other countries of the world, but not often in the United States.

# Parents in Prison

Some librarians across the country have started developing programs for children whose parents are in prison. When an adult was out on the street dealing drugs or involved in other criminal activity, concern for family may not have been that parent's top priority. When the same persons are given a long jail term, it is not unusual for them to start thinking about the children in their life and develop a desire to help them get the tools they need to succeed. Because of this, early literacy programs have sprung up in prisons. Geared for adults who already know how to read and write, these programs teach the adults the importance of early exposure to books in a positive way and give them tools for using books with children.

In some cases, the prisons ask local librarians to provide regular early literacy programs such as preschool storytimes. In other cases, when physical contact between the prisoner and his family is not allowed or if the family lives too far away for frequent visits, some programs encourage the prisoner to read a book aloud and record it. The recording is then sent to the young relative, along with a copy of the book. The children can then experience their adult reading a book aloud to them, even if they are not in the same location. In addition, having shared a book together gives a ready topic for conversation in phone calls that might otherwise be stilted.

Librarians should make sure that that the parent or caregiver is aware of this program and willing to use this service. Keep in mind that the incarcerated adult may not have treated family members and others well. Having a tape sent may be a reminder of traumatic times. Once a child's family knows that this service is available, respect their decision to decline, if they so choose.

Some librarians extend their summer reading programs into the prisons by allowing children to sign up during visits to their incarcerated relatives. At the end of the summer, a final party with refreshments and completion certificates takes place in the prison. The incarcerated adult can joyfully celebrate with their child, making the prison visit a positive experience for everyone.

# Homeless Children

Parents of children living in homeless shelters may not want them to borrow books; there could be a greater possibility of overdue fines and lost books when a residence is only temporary. Care should be taken to assure the parents that reading to their child is very important and that they can return the book at the next storytime session. These children might also have difficulty holding on to a Summer Reading Club game board. Offer to allow these children to keep their game board at the library if they are worried about losing it.

Homeless children may come into the children's room with their caregiver and stay for hours, because the public library is one of the few places they can go during that day that has air-conditioning in the hot summer and heat in the wintertime. The children's room may provide a wonderful refuge for both parent and child; it is especially important to remember to be welcoming to these families.

## Summary

All children should be made to feel that the children's room is their space. It should be a nonjudgmental environment where children are free to be children, where their imaginations are nurtured and their love for books and stories is encouraged. No matter what the situation, the librarian can strive to make the public library experience for each child as positive as possible.

# CHAPTER 10

## Special Events

Children and their families often enjoy coming to special events at the public library as well as to regular storytimes. Holidays can be used as the backdrop for these events, as can authors' birthdays, local happenings, and manufactured events. For instance, each year, the Children's Book Council runs Children's Book Week. This is a time when librarians typically bring in authors or illustrators and run more than the usual amount of programs for children. There is National Poetry Month during which poetry can be brought into preschools, and El día de los niños/El día de los libros (Día), which is a multicultural celebration of children, families, and reading.

The purpose of these events is to bring people into the library, to give them a new and joyous experience in the library, and to plant in them the sense that the library is such a wonderful place, they will want to come back and visit again and again. To do this, it is important not to rely only on tried and true programs, but to extend yourself by trying new programs and using new partners to expand the programs that the library has to offer.

## Ways to Bring People to the Library

People who already come to the library are the ones who will be familiar with the notices and flyers that are posted regularly within the library. Therefore, if you want to attract a new audience to the library, it makes sense to advertise *outside* the traditional library network.

If looking for an audience for preschool programs, you may want to start by forging a connection with local preschools; ask the teachers to remind parents to take their children to the library and, if you have flyers for a particular event, be sure to bring them to the preschool for distribution to families. Walk through your neighborhood and ask owners of local businesses frequented by families with preschoolers if you can leave flyers on the counter or display a flyer in their window. Bring a tape dispenser and plenty of flyers with you. Eating establishments, especially pizza, ice cream, and fast food, as well as toy stores and places that sell diapers, are good places to visit. As mentioned in Chapter Eight, having beauty salons post notices may reach some mothers.

Other places to advertise are local churches, doctors' offices, and government offices where parents may go for a variety of information needs. Asking the local elementary school to put a notice in its newsletter to parents may reach homes where the siblings of the school-age children are preschool children.

It may be helpful to ask people who are interested in attending preschool programs to call the library. This will provide some indication of the numbers to expect and the size of the facility it will take to accommodate those who wish to attend.

## El día de los niños/El día de los libros

Often referred to simply as "Día" and celebrated annually on April 30, Pat Mora's enhancement of the Children's Day celebration that began in 1925 has become a multicultural celebration of children, families, and reading. Celebrations often joyfully include music, food, and lots of book connections. Spanish-language storytellers, bilingual storytimes, musical performances, and street fairs with local merchants are just some types of Día community-wide celebrations. The Association for Library Services to Children (ALSC) maintains a Web site devoted to Día providing free downloadable brochures, logos, bibliographies, articles, program suggestions, and links. A sample toolkit and attendee survey were also available at the time this book was being written. The site also has links to awards for Spanish-language books. Another link allows libraries to add information about their Día celebrations; viewers can find events in their local areas by clicking on an interactive map of the United States. For more information about Día, visit http://www.ala.org/ala/mgrps/divs/alsc/initiatives/diadelosninos/index.cfm

# Festivals and Celebrations

Establishing a tradition of a festival or celebration builds rapport with the library, and it is never too early to start the process. Asking parents to bring their children to such an event may entice them to join the library and obtain checkout privileges for the entire family, thus helping older siblings become library patrons. One may be tempted to do a really large event and then find it too overwhelming, only to never do another. Starting with a smaller event or with one with which you have a lot of help is a good beginning. Festivals can center around a local hero, a national holiday, the publication of a popular book (such as when the Harry Potter books were released), or any event.

# Community Festivals

Holding community festivals in the library is a way to bring people in, unite the community, and promote library services without having to spend much money on advertising. Storytelling festivals, poetry contests, National Black History month, and book week celebrations all lend themselves to library-sponsored events. If your library has a large open space, invite community groups to run tables. Set up tables around the perimeter of the open area, and give each organization a table and two chairs. Each organization is responsible for some type of activity that children of all ages can take part in, but there should also be specific things that preschool children can do while standing at the table. This can include coloring, gluing, cutting, sorting, pasting, and folding. While running the activity, the sponsoring agency can also display handout materials with information regarding their specific organization.

If a group is happy to run a table but does not know what to do, a few suggestions include origami, face painting, or decorating a cutout shape such as a mitten or a star. If you have permission to bring live animals into the library, you may want to invite a member of the nearest 4H club to bring in a rabbit for children to pet. While they are petting the rabbit, the person in charge can answer questions about rabbit care.

You may also want to create your own events. For instance, each year, the Enoch Pratt Free Library hosts a Fairy Tale Festival. A kickoff at their Central Library is followed by an entire month of related activities at all of the branches. A *Fairy Tale Gazette* is published that lists all of the events during the month throughout the library kingdom. Programs may include storytelling with folktales, magic shows, and tea parties. The key to holding successful, large celebrations is finding community partners who are willing to take responsibility for one program or activity. You can serve as the coordinator for the event, rather than being a staff person assigned to just one particular area. Some type of complication always arises, so for smooth functioning of the event, it is imperative to have at least one person without set responsibilities to act as the troubleshooter and to fill in at different tables as needed.

Although you may not be able to undertake such a grand event, you could offer a Fairy Tale Festival for preschool children where they come to storytime dressed as fairy tale characters. You can offer storytelling featuring royal characters or fairies. Perhaps a student from a local high school who would like to show off a few magic tricks. Smaller children are often, but not always, easy to fool. Certainly it is possible to have a royal tea party, with or without real tea. Children love pretending they are drinking tea and eating cookies, and this is even more exciting if they are encouraged to imagine that they are in the presence of a queen. Imagination is powerful; a royal tea party is even possible using a one-dimensional cup, teapot, and cookies that children create from paper, crayons, scissors, and paste.

# Summer Reading Clubs

Studies suggest that children will have a much easier time retaining their reading skills if they read over the summer rather than take a total break from reading at the end of one school year until the beginning of another. But how can children be enticed to read during the summer, if they don't *have to*?

A wise librarian invented Summer Reading Clubs. Many different manifestations of this odd beast appear each summer, but they all have the same underlying principle. Read lots of books during the summer and feel proud of yourself! How is this accomplished?

Summer Reading Clubs were originally geared toward readers, and thus most prereading preschoolers were excluded from the group of players. Because research shows that being read to in the early years is a great way to help children develop a vocabulary and familiarity with books that will help them be successful in school, Summer Reading Clubs have evolved and now most have a component geared for nonreaders under age five. By 2000, many libraries opened registration to children who were being read to rather than limiting registration to children who could read to themselves. This meant that children under age three could participate. Parents were thus encouraged to begin reading to their babies as well as their young children. Through this new policy, librarians hoped that the promise of a prize for reading so many books would encourage families to read aloud together, leading to a lifetime habit of reading (Celano and Neuman, 2001).

Planning such events has become very simple. Librarians in some state library associations began planning summer reading program themes together, buying incentives at bulk rates and then distributing them to individual libraries within the state. When planning at the state level, bulk orders of materials made it much less expensive for smaller libraries to purchase giveaways for their participants. There was no need for a multitude of libraries to worry about spending time and creative energy looking for ready-made incentives or developing them in-house. The choices provided by the state library were items that matched the Summer Reading Club theme, were safe for children, and were age-appropriate.

The time and money saved through such collaboration was so significant that many state libraries decided to embrace a national Summer Reading Program with a common theme and accompanying materials. The incentives, written material describing program ideas, and accompanying CDs with music or downloadable graphics are extras that need to be purchased. In some states, the library association pays the cost; in others, individual librarians must buy it, sometimes at a reduced cost. However, the program takes all the step-by-step planning away and provides a well-thought-out, polished, and graphically appealing finished product.

Some children's librarians still prefer to develop their own Summer Reading Program. They may ask for volunteers in the community to help design graphics, for local merchants to donate incentives, and for teenagers to register Summer Reading participants as well as record the books read.

Before the school year ends, librarians might visit local schools and childcare centers with registration applications. After explaining the Summer Reading Club (SRC) rules, displaying some exciting incentives, and perhaps reading a book aloud, the librarian collects the applications that have been completed by the teachers (or the students, if they are older than preschool). In the summertime, children across the United States are encouraged to sign up for the SRC at their local library. Advertising for SRC registration can be done at the end of each storytime session, or through posters in the library. Children may be able to register online or by filling out a form in person.

Once children have registered, they are usually given something, such as a game board, a list, or written instructions for the game. These materials often contain an unfilled list with lines on which the child can record all of the books they have listened to or read by themselves. To avoid confusion, there may be different game boards for children who are already readers and for preschoolers who are still at the "read to me" stage. But the message is clear: reading in the summertime benefits everyone!

In the past, when librarians had more time and fewer participants, they might ask each child, "Tell me what you liked about the book. Tell me what you didn't." This was a way to ensure that the child really read the book. However, this is labor intensive, and young children are generally unable to articulate their opinions regarding the books. Thus, in most libraries, this practice of requiring verbal or written book reports has been phased out.

## Author and Illustrator Programs

Although preschoolers are generally too young to read on their own, they can learn the names of their favorite authors and illustrators. Inviting children's authors or illustrators to read their book aloud or even to sign copies of their books for your public can be similar to hosting a rock-and-roll festival for a teenager. Make sure you have plenty of copies of the works on hand, and encourage the families to borrow books once the presentation has ended.

## Booking Performers

Hiring performers was covered in Chapter Two, but it's worth mentioning more on the topic here because most sessions with outside performers are a special event. When it is not possible or preferable to present your own program, you may be asked to book an outside performer. First, find out how much money you have available for the event. Taking limited funds into account, you may find it helpful to call a colleague and find out if he or she can recommend anyone local for your program. When speaking with the performer, give a selection of dates and find out if this person is available at any of the times. Remind your performer to think of the ages of the children who will be at the performance and what they would enjoy. Too many programs have been led astray by a storyteller who was performing for kids above the grade level of the audience. Make sure that the performer knows that he or she will be facing an audience of preschoolers, and a silly poem should be chosen rather than a soliloquy by Shakespeare.

After finding out what the performer charges, ask if there is a reduced price for more than one performance. If you are in a small library, you may want to "share" the performer with another small library or hire the performer to do some school visits for you. If the performer does not have a contract, send out one of yours. Decide if you will be reimbursing for mileage. Check with your local educational council to see if you can get continuing education unit certificates to hand out if the performer is a teacher for adult educators. Ask your performer to send any digital photographs or Web site links that can be included with your advertising, both in print and online.

# Flexibility

One of the most important attributes of a children's librarian is flexibility. How do you demonstrate flexibility? What happens if you are invaded by a class of ten rowdy three year olds from a home day care? You may have been expecting a quiet afternoon when you hoped to catch up on professional reading, and instead you find yourself running after children who seem to enjoy pulling books off the shelves and treating the library as a playground. Rather than futilely trying to keep order, the best way to deal with this is to offer a program that you have presented before and is still fresh in your mind, make one up on the spot, or have a ready-to-go program for situations such as these. Tell a story, read one that requires interaction, and include a song that most children are familiar with such as "The Wheels on the Bus" or "If You're Happy and You Know It." Using this formula, you will find more children with focused attention than if you stood in front of them and had shouted for quiet over and over. Nothing gains a child's' attention better than simply singing a song that they already know and can participate in. And a good book, read well, can always draw an appreciative audience.

# Final Words

While children's librarians for preschoolers may not have the largest salaries, the position can be hugely rewarding. You always have new children to meet, new books to discover and pass on to your patrons, and new programs to present to an eager audience. You can help children recognize letters and numbers, thus becoming ready for school. You can share your love of books with children so that they learn to love them, too. You can encourage caregivers to interact joyously with their children and provide materials that will give guidance. In the children's room, you can create a welcoming place for preschoolers where they can connect, imagine, and explore. Perhaps best of all, you can watch your preschoolers grow out of preschool storytime and happily move on to become children who succeed in kindergarten.

# Appendix A
# Nursery Rhyme Suggestions

Following is a list of nursery rhyme collections, all with large illustrations that are great for showing to a group as you recite the rhymes.

Ada, Alma Flo, F. Isabel Campoy, and Alice Schertle. *¡Pío Peep!* New York: HarperCollins, 2003.

Beaton, Clare. *Mother Goose Remembers*. Cambridge: Barefoot Books, 2006.

Cousins, Lucy. *The Little Dog Laughed and Other Nursery Rhymes*. New York: Macmillan Children's Books, 1989.

Crews, Nina. *The Neighborhood Mother Goose* (ALA Notable Children's Books; Younger Readers [awards]). New York: Amistad, 2004.

Faurot, Kimberly. *Mother Goose Rhyme Time Animals*. Ft. Atkinson, WI: Upstart Books, 2006.

Gustafson, Scott. *Favorite Nursery Rhymes from Mother Goose*. Hartford, CT: The Greenwich Workshop Press, 2007.

Hudson, Cheryl Willis. *Many Colors of Mother Goose*. New York: Just Us Books, 2000.

Larche, Doug. *Father Gander Nursery Rhymes*. Santa Barbara, CA: Advocacy Press, 1986.

Opie, Iona, ed. *Here Comes Mother Goose (My Very First Mother Goose)*. Cambridge, MA: Candlewick, 1999.

Yaccarino, Dan. *Dan Yaccarino's Mother Goose*. New York: Random House Children's Books, 2004.

# Appendix B
# Professional Materials for Planning Children's Programming

Association for Library Services to Children. *The Newbery and Caldecott Awards: A Guide to the Medal of Honor Books, 2010 Edition.* Chicago: American Library Association, 2010.

Association for Library Services to Children, Association for Library Trustees and Advocates, Public Library Association. *Unattended Children in the Public Library: A Resource Guide.* Chicago: American Library Association, 2000.

Bailey, Becky A. *I Love You Rituals.* New York: HarperCollins, 2000. (These great adaptations of well-known songs and rhymes provide an opportunity for parent–child bonding.)

Bauer, Carolyn. *Leading Kids to Books through Crafts* (Mighty Easy Motivator Series). Chicago: ALA Editions, 2000.

Bauer, Carolyn. *Leading Kids to Books through Magic* (Mighty Easy Motivator Series). Chicago: ALA Editions, 1996.

Bauer, Carolyn. *Leading Kids to Books through Puppets* (Mighty Easy Motivator Series). Chicago: ALA Editions, 1997.

Bauer, Carolyn. *This Way to Books.* New York: H.W. Wilson, 1983.

Birckmayer, Jennifer, Anne Stonehouse, and Anne Kennedy. *From Lullabies to Literature: Stories in the Lives of Infants and Toddlers.* Washington, DC: NAEYC, 2008.

Bradbury, Judy. *Children's Book Corner: A Read Aloud Resource with Tips, Techniques, and Plans for Teachers, Librarians and Parents Level Pre-K–K.* Westport, CT: Libraries Unlimited, 2003.

Bromann, Jennifer. *More Storytime Action: 2000+ Ideas for Making 500+Picture Books Active.* New York: Neal Schuman, 2009.

Carlow, Regina. *Exploring the Connection between Children's Literature and Music.* Westport, CT: Libraries Unlimited, 2008. (For the librarian who would like to use music with children but feels less than competent to do so.)

Carlson, Ann. *Flannelboard Stories for Infants and Toddlers.* Chicago: American Library Association, 1999.

Carlson, Ann D. *Concept Books and Young Children.* http://comminfo.rutgers.edu/professional-development/childlit/books/CARLSON.pdf. Accessed December 18, 2009.

Cass-Beggs, Barbara. *Your Baby Needs Music*. North Vancouver, BC: Douglas & McIntyre, 1978. (The "Listen, Like, Learn approach" is explained. Songs that have been collected, written, or adapted for children from birth to age two are included with musical notation.)

Cass-Beggs, Barbara. *Your Child Needs Music*. Mississauga, Canada: The Frederick Harris Music Co., 1986. (The time-tested techniques for teaching music to preschoolers include use of music instruments, colored scarves, and creative dramatics. These individual segments can be used successfully within any preschool program.)

Celano, D., & Neuman, S.B. *The role of public libraries in children's literacy development: An evaluation report.* Harrisburg, PA: Pennsylvania Library Association, 2001.

Cerny, Rosanne, Penny Markey, and Amanda Williams. *Outstanding Library Service to Children: Putting the Core Competencies to Work.* Chicago: American Library Association, 2006.

*The Children's Book of Alphabets*. New York: The Chicken House Scholastic, 2002.

Codell, Esme Raji. *How to Get Your Children to Love Reading for Ravenous and Reluctant Readers Alike: Activities, Ideas, and Inspiration for Exploring Everything in the World through Books.* Chapel Hill, NC: Algonquin Books of Chapel Hill, 2003. (Written by the author of *Educating Esme.*)

Cohen, Arlene. *Stories on the Move: Integrating Literature and Movement with Children from Infants to Age 14.* Westport, CT: Libraries Unlimited, 2007. (The first 81 pages of this 226-page book focus on preschool activities.)

Cullum, Carolyn. *The Storytime Sourcebook Bundle*. New York: Neal Schuman, 2008.

Deeds, Sharon, and Catherine Chastain, eds. *New Books Kids Like*. Chicago: American Library Association, 2001.

De Las Casas, Diane. *Handmade Tales: Stories to Make and Take.* Westport, CT: Libraries Unlimited, 2008.

Diamant-Cohen, Betsy. *Children's Services: Partnerships for Success.* Chicago: ALA Editions, 2010.

Diamant-Cohen, Betsy. *Early Literacy Programming en Español: Mother Goose on the Loose Programs for Bilingual Learners.* Book and CD-ROM edition. New York: Neal-Schuman, 2010.

Diamant-Cohen, Betsy. *Mother Goose on the Loose: A Handbook and CD-ROM Kit with Scripts, Rhymes, Songs, Flannel-Board Patterns and Activities.* New York: Neal Schuman, 2006.

Diamant-Cohen, Betsy, and Saroj Nadkarni Ghoting. *The Early Literacy Kit: A Handbook and Tip Cards.* Chicago: American Library Association, 2009.

Diamond, Jonathan, Katie Laris, Joanne Woodward, the Child Development Institute (Bronxville, NY), and Jonathan Diamond Associates. *When a Child Pretends: Understanding Pretend Play.* New York: Jonathan Diamond Associates, 2006. DVD.

East, Kathy A., and Rebecca L. Thomas. *Across Cultures: A Guide to Multicultural Literature for Children.* Westport, CT: Libraries Unlimited, 2007.

Ernst, Linda L. *Body Rhyming Time.* New York: Neal Schuman, 2008.

Faurot, Kimberly K. *Books in Bloom: Creative Patterns and Props that Bring Stories to Life.* Chicago: American Library Association, 2003.

Faurot, Kimberly K. *Mother Goose Rhyme Time.* Fort Atkinson, WI: Upstart Books, 2006. (A wonderful series with topics on animals, people, and night. Includes rhyme lyrics, flannel board pieces and templates, early literacy activities, storytime ideas, extension ideas, and take-home reproducibles.)

Feinberg, Sandra, Joan E. Kuchner, and Sari Feldman. *Learning Environments for Young Children: Rethinking Library Spaces and Services.* Chicago: American Library Association, 1998. (This 8 x 11 inch book includes much white space in the margins. Part I, "Essential Elements for Learning," includes "Family Centered and Developmentally Appropriate Practice" [11 pages], "The Social Environment [16 pages], "Physical Environment" [13 pages], "Parent Participation," [16 pages], "Collaboration and Networks" [10 pages], and "Professional Development" [9 pages]. The parent participation part includes topics such as parents as critical friends, advocates, and partners in the educational process, as well as linking parents to resources. Another section in this part is "Parent Education and Support." Part II is titled "The Early Childhood Quality Review." Part III covers "Quality Review Tools" with four appendixes of tools.)

Folini, Melissa Rossetti. *Story Times Good Enough to Eat! Thematic Programs with Edible Story Crafts.* Santa Barbara, CA: Libraries Unlimited, 2010.

Fox, Mem. *Reading Magic: Why Reading Aloud to Our Children Will Change Their Lives Forever.* Illustrated by Judy Horacek. San Diego, CA: A Harvest Original Harcourt, 2001.

Fredericks, Anthony D. *Mother Goose Readers Theatre for Beginning Readers.* Westport, CT: Teacher Ideas Press, 2007. (Fredericks is a prolific writer of excellent resources to share with teachers. His readers theater collection may be of more use in the school library than the public library, but check out the ideas.)

Fredericks, Anthony D. *Songs and Rhymes Readers Theatre for Beginning Readers.* Westport, CT: Teacher Ideas Press, 2007.

Freeman, Judy. *Books Kids Will Sit Still For: A Read-Aloud Guide* (3 vols.). Westport, CT: Libraries Unlimited, 2006.

Freeman, Judy. *Once Upon a Time: Using Storytelling, Creative Drama, and Reader's Theater with Children in Grades PreK–6.* Westport, CT: Libraries Unlimited, 2007.

Ghoting, Saroj Nadkarni, and Pamela Martin-Diaz. *Early Literacy Storytimes @ Your Library: Partnering with Caregivers for Success.* Chicago: American Library Association, 2006. (Section titles include "Learning It!" with chapters on explaining early literacy research, incorporating and explaining key early literacy concepts, talking about how to read, how to make storytime meaningful, and a part on teaching English as a second language and early literacy. The Section on "Doing It!" goes into planning for storytimes and gives sample storytimes for early talkers, talkers, and prereaders and then talks about building storytimes. Section III, "Keeping It Going!" discusses assessing and promoting storytimes. The appendixes include a page of the "Manual Alphabet" without explanation for why it is there. Appendix B is "Encouraging Literacy at Home" and has sample parent tip take-home pages.)

Gopnik, Alison, Patricia K. Kuhl, and Andrew N. Meltzoff. *The Scientist in the Crib: What Early Learning Tells Us about the Mind.* Brattleboro, VT: Harper Paperbacks, 2001.

Greene, Ellin, and Janice M. Del Negro. *Storytelling: Art & Technique.* Santa Barbara, CA: Libraries Unlimited, 2010.

Haven, Kendall, and MaryGay Ducy. *Crash Course in Storytelling.* Westport, CT: Libraries Unlimited, 2006.

Hirsh-Pasek, Kathy, and Roberta Michnick Golinkoff, with Diane Eyer. *Einstein Never Used Flashcards: How Our Children Really Learn—and Why They Need to Play More and Memorize Less.* Emmaus, PA: Rodale Books, 2003.

Hornburg, Val Z. *On the Wing of a Whitebird: A Tomie dePaola Resource Book.* Westport, CT: Teacher Ideas Press, an Imprint of Libraries Unlimited, 2005.

Horning, Kathleen T. *From Cover to Cover*, rev. ed. New York: HarperCollins, 2010.

Immroth, Barbara Froeling, and Viki Ash-Geisler. *Achieving School Readiness: Public Libraries and National Education. With a Prototype of Public Library Services for Young Children and Their Families.* Chicago: American Library Association, 1995.

Irving, Jan, and Robin Currie. *Mudluscious: Stories and Activities Featuring Food for Preschool Children.* Westport, CT: Libraries Unlimited, 1986.

Jalongo, Mary. *Young Children and Picture Books,* 2nd ed. Washington, DC: National Association for the Education of Young Children, 2004.

Jurenka, Nancy Allen. *Teaching Phonemic Awareness through Children's Literature.* Westport, CT: Teacher Ideas Press, 2005.

Keane, Nancy J. *The Big Book of Children's Reading Lists: 100 Great, Ready-to-Use Book Lists for Educators, Librarians, Parents, and Children.* Westport, CT: Libraries Unlimited, 2006.

Lakovakis, Laurel L. *Puppet Plays Plus: Using Stock Characters to Entertain and Teach Early Literacy.* Westport, CT: 2009.

Langemack, Chapple. *The Author Event Primer: How to Plan, Execute and Enjoy Author Events.* Westport, CT: Libraries Unlimited, 2007.

Lima, Carolyn W., and Rebecca L. Thomas. *A to Zoo: Subject Access to Children's Picture Books Supplement to the 7th Edition* (Children's and Young Adult Literature Reference). Westport, CT: Libraries Unlimited, 2008.

Lipman, Doug. *Improving Your Storytelling: Beyond the Basics for All Who Tell Stories in Work and Play.* Atlanta, GA: August House, 1999.

Low, Elizabeth Cothen. *Big Book of Animal Rhymes, Fingerplays, and Songs.* Westport, CT: Libraries Unlimited, 2009.

Lowe, Joy L., and Kathyn Matthew. *Puppet Magic.* New York: Neal Schuman, 2008.

MacDonald, Margaret Read. *Booksharing: 101 Programs to Use with Preschoolers.* Hamden, CT: Library Professional Publications, 1988. (The table of contents might help you organize your own collection of programs. Sections include "Science Beginnings" [Habitats, Exploring Your Backyard, How Things Work, Young Scientists, Geological Wonders, Exploring Our Senses, and Basic Concepts], "Through the Year: Seasons" [Fall, Winter, Spring, Summer], "Celebrations" [Valentine's Day, St. Patrick's Day, April Fool's Day, Easter, May Day, Arbor Day, Fourth of July, Halloween, Thanksgiving, Hanukkah, Christmas, and Birthdays], "Getting to Know Yourself" [Feelings, About You: Making Faces, Sleepy Storytime, New Shoes, etc.], "Using Your Imagination" [Adventuring], "Animal Antics" [Happy Lions, Crocodiles and Alligators, Mice Are Nice, Portly Pigs, Problem Pups], "Dreams and Nonsense," "Ethnic Programs," and "Art Concepts Series Focus on Art, Music and Time".)

MacDonald, Margaret Read. *Storytellers Start-Up Book.* Atlanta, GA: August House, 1993.

MacMillan, Kathy. *A Box Full of Tales: Easy Ways to Share Library Resources through Story Boxes.* Chicago: ALA Editions, 2008.

MacMillan, Kathy. *Try Your Hand at This: Easy Ways to Incorporate Sign Language into Your Programs.* New York: Scarecrow Press, 2006.

Marks, Diane F. *Children's Book Award Handbook.* Westport, CT: Libraries Unlimited, 2006.

Matulka, Denise I. *A Picture Book Primer: Understanding and Using Picture Books.* Westport, CT: Libraries Unlimited, 2008.

Minkel, Walter. *How to Do "The Three Bears" with Two Hands: Performing with Puppets.* Chicago: American Library Association, 2003.

Morgan, Judith, and Neil Morgan. *Dr. Seuss & Mr. Geisel: A Biography.* New York: Random House, 1995.

National Scientific Council on the Developing Child. *Young Children Develop in an Environment of Relationships: Working Paper No. 1.* Cambridge, MA, Harvard University, 2004.

Nespeca, Sue McCleaf, and Joan B. Reeve. *Picture Books Plus: 100 Extension Activities in Art, Drama, Music, Math, and Science.* Chicago: American Library Association, 2003.

Nichols, Judy. *Storytimes for Two-Year-Olds.* Chicago: ALA Editions, 2007.

Nickse, Ruth S., and Shelley Quezada. *Community Collaborations for Family Literacy Handbook.* New York: Neal-Schuman, 1993.

Peck, Penny. *Crash Course in Children's Services.* Westport, CT: Libraries Unlimited, 2006.

Pilger, Mary Ann. *Multicultural Projects Index: Things to Make and Do to Celebrate Festivals, Culture, and Holidays around the World.* Westport, CT: Libraries Unlimited, 2005.

Pixton, Kaaren. Indestructibles (series). New York: Workman, 2009–2010. (This series of indestructible books made of a paper-like material includes *Creep! Crawl!; Flutter! Fly!; Wiggle! March!;* and *Jungle, Rumble!*)

Polette, Nancy. *Find Some Who: Introducing 200 Favorite Picture Books.* Westport, CT: Libraries Unlimited, 2006. (Nancy Polette is a prolific writer who has many great ideas to share. Please check her books in the professional literature catalogs for many more sure winners.)

Raines, Shirley, Karen Miller, and Leah Curry-Rood. *Story S-t-r-e-t-c-h-e-r-s® for Infants, Toddlers: Experiences, Activities, and Games for Popular Children's Books.* Bethesda, MD: Gryphon House, 2002. (Great ideas for activities that go along with specific books can be found in any of the Story Stretcher series.)

Reid, Rob. *Children's Jukebox, Second Edition: The Select Subject Guide to Children's Musical Recordings.* Chicago: ALA Editions, 2007.

Reid, Rob. *Shake and Shout.* Janesville, WI: Upstart, 2008. (All of the above three books by Rob Reid give creative ideas and suggest resources for adding music to library programs.)

Reid, Rob. *Something Musical Happened at the Library: Adding Song and Dance to Children's Story Programs.* Chicago: ALA Editions, 2007.

Silberg, Jackie; and Pam Schiller. *The Complete Book of Rhymes, Songs, Poems, Fingerplays and Chants: Over 700 Selections [With 2 CDs with 50 Songs].* Beltsville, MD: Gryphon House, 2006.

Sipe, Lawrence R. *Storytime: Young Children's Literary Understanding in the Classroom* (Language and Literacy). New York: Teachers College Press, 2007.

Sitarz, Paula Gaj. *More Picture Book Story Hours.* Englewood, CO: Libraries Unlimited, 1990.

Snow, Sharon. *Building Blocks: Building a Parent-Child Literacy Program at the Library.* Westport, CT: Libraries Unlimited, 2007. (The author of this book worked at a test site for the ALSC program "Every Child a Reader." She combines her experience with a reading readiness program in a branch library in San Jose and offers an introduction to a structured program for parents and children.)

Steele, Anitra T. *Bare Bones Children's Services: Tips for Library Generalists.* Chicago: Association for Library Service to Children, American Library Association, 2001.

Sullivan, Michael. *Fundamentals of Children's Services.* Chicago: American Library Association, 2005.

Taylor-Dileva, Kimberly. *Once Upon a Sign: Using American Sign Language to Engage, Entertain, and Teach All Children.* Santa Barbara, CA: Libraries Unlimited, 2010.

Trelease, Jim. *The Read Aloud Handbook*, 6th ed. New York: Penguin Books, 2006. (Jim Trelease has been a much-sought-after speaker as well as the author of this "bible" for reading aloud to children. Although the focus is for parents, the librarian can use his suggestions for program planning as well as to share with interested parents.)

Trevino, Rose Zertuche (ed.). *The Pura Belpre Awards: Celebrating Latino Authors and Illustrators.* Washington, DC: American Library Association, 2006.

Trevino, Rose Zertuche. *Read Me a Rhyme in Spanish and English/Léame una rima en español e ingles.* Chicago: American Library Association, 2009.

Vardell, Sylvia M. *Poetry Aloud Here!* Chicago: ALA, 2006.

Wadham, Tim. *Libros Esenciales Building, Marketing, and Programming a Core Collection of Spanish Language Children's Materials.* New York: Neal Schuman, 2007.

Walter, Virginia A. *Children & Libraries: Getting It Right.* Washington, DC: American Library Association, 2001.

Wells, Rosemary. *My Shining Star: Raising a Child Who Is Ready to Learn.* New York: Scholastic, 2006.

Yolen, Jane. *This Little Piggy and Other Rhymes to Sing and Play: Lap Songs, Finger Plays, Clapping Games, and Pantomime Rhymes.* Illustrated by Will Hillenbrand. Cambridge, MA: Candlewick Press, 2005.

Zahniser, Elizabeth Lund. *The Music Box: Songs, Rhymes, and Games for Young Children.* Wellesley, MA: ELZ Publishing, 2006.

Zigler, Edward, Dorothy G. Singer, and Sandra J. Bishop-Josef, eds. *Children's Play: The Roots of Reading.* Washington, DC: Zero to Three, 2004.

Zingher, Gary. *Theme Play: Exciting Young Imaginations.* Westport, CT: Libraries Unlimited, 2006.

# Appendix C
# Picture Books Mentioned in This Book

Ackerman Grant, Judyann. *Chicken Said, "Cluck!"* New York: HarperCollins, 2008.

Arnold, Tedd. *Super Fly*. New York: Scholastic, 2007.

Bang, Molly. *The Grey Lady and the Strawberry Snatcher*. New York: Simon & Schuster, 1980.

Berenstain, Jan, and Mike Berenstain. *The Berenstain Bears Go Out to Eat*. New York: HarperFestival, 2010.

Brown, Marcia. *Stone Soup*. New York: Aladdin, 1997.

Browne, Anthony. *Hansel and Gretel*. New York: Walker Books, 2008.

Buehner, Caralyn. *Goldilocks and the Three Bears*. New York: Dial, 2007.

Carle, Eric. *The Very Busy Spider*. New York: Scholastic, 1996.

Cimarusti, Marie Torres. *Peek-a-Choo-Choo!* New York: Dutton Juvenile, 2007.

Cole, Babette. *Prince Cinders*. New York: Putnam Juvenile, 1997.

Cousins, Lucy. *Maisy Goes to Bed*. New York: Little, Brown & Co., 1990.

Crews, Donald. *Freight Train Big Book* (Mulberry Big Book). New York: HarperTrophy, 1993.

Demas, Corinne. *Always in Trouble*. New York: Scholastic Press, 2009.

Dewdney, Anna. *Llama, Llama Red Pajama*. New York: Scholastic, 2005.

Dr. Seuss. *The Cat in the Hat*. New York. Random House, 1985 [©1957].

Feiffer, Jules. *Bark, George*. New York: HarperCollins, 2000.

Fleischman, Paul. *Glass Slipper, Gold Sandal A Worldwide Cinderella*. New York: Henry Holt Books for Young Readers, 2007.

Foley, Greg. *Don't Worry Bear*. New York: Viking Juvenile, 2008.

Freeman, Don. *Corduroy 40th Anniversary Edition*. New York: Viking Juvenile, 2008.

Galdone, Paul. *The Three Little Pigs*. New York: Clarion Books, 2006.

Gerstein, Mordicai. *The Man Who Walked between the Towers*. New York: Henry Holt, 2003.

Grimm, Brothers. *Rapunzel* (Picture Puffin Books). New York: Puffin, 2002.

Harper, Wilhelmina. *The Gunniwolf*. New York: Dutton Juvenile, 2003.

Hazen, Barbara Shook. *Tight Times*. New York: Puffin, 1983.

Hill, Susan. *Ruby Bakes a Cake* (I Can Read!/Ruby Raccoon). Grand Rapids, MI: Zonderkidz, 2010.

Hoban, Tana. *Circles, Triangles and Squares*. New York: Simon & Schuster Children's Publishing, 1974.

Hoban, Tana. *Count and See*. New York: Simon & Schuster Children's Publishing, 1972.

Hoban, Tana. *More, Fewer, Less*. New York: Greenwillow, 1998.

Hoban, Tana. *Push, Pull, Empty, Full: A Book of Opposites*. New York: Collier Books, 1976.

Hutchins, Pat. *Rosie's Walk*. New York: Scholastic, 1987.

Isadora, Rachel. *Peekaboo Bedtime*. New York: Putnam Juvenile, 2008.

Kalan, Robert. *Jump, Frog, Jump! Board Book*. New York: HarperFestival, 2003.

Keats, Ezra Jack. *Peter's Chair*. New York: Viking Juvenile, 1998.

Kimmel, Eric A. *Anansi and the Moss-Covered Rock*. New York: Holiday House, 1990.

Krensky, Stephen. *Bubble Trouble* (Ready-to-Read Level 1). New York: Aladdin, 2004.

Lamm, C. Drew. *The Prog Frince*. New York: Scholastic, 1999.

Lears, Laurie. *Ian's Walk: A Story about Autism*. Morton Grove, IL: Albert Whitman & Company, 2003.

Levine, Michelle. *Giant Pandas* (Pull Ahead Books). Minneapolis, MN: Lerner Publications, 2006.

Martin, Bill Jr. *Brown Bear, Brown Bear, What Do You See? Anniversary Edition*. New York: Henry Holt, 2008.

Meyer, Mercer. *A Boy, a Dog, and a Frog*. New York: Dial, 2003.

Munsch, Robert. *Alligator Baby*. New York: Cartwheel, 2002.

Munsch, Robert. *Angela's Airplane*. Toronto: Annick Press, 1986.

Numeroff, Laura Joffe. *If You Give a Mouse a Cookie* (If You Give . . .). New York: Laura Geringer, 1985.

Partridge, Elizabeth. *Big Cat Pepper*. New York: Bloomsbury USA Children's Books, 2009.

Pixton, Kaaren. *Indestructibles Creep! Crawl!* Chicago: Workman, 2009.

Pixton, Kaaren. *Indestructibles Flutter! Fly!* Chicago: Workman, 2009.

Pixton, Kaaren. *Indestructibles Wiggle! March!* Chicago: Workman, 2009.

Rathmann, Peggy. *Officer Buckle and Gloria*. New York: Putnam & Sons, 1995.

Root, Phyllis. *One Duck Stuck*. Cambridge, MA: Candlewick, 2003.

San Souci, Robert D. *Cendrillion: A Caribbean Cinderella*. New York: Turtleback Books, 2002.

Scieszka, Jon. *The Frog Prince, Continued* (Picture Puffin). New York City: Puffin, 1994.

Scieszka, Jon. *The True Story of the Three Little Pigs*. New York City: Puffin, 1996.

Scieszka, Jon. *The Stinky Cheese Man and Other Fairly Stupid Tales*. New York: Viking Juvenile, 1992.

Shaw, Charles. *It Looked Like Spilt Milk* (Big Book Edition). New York: HarperCollins, 1992.

Slobodkina, Esphyr. *Caps for Sale*. New York: Harper Collins, 1968.

Tarcov, Edith H. *The Frog Prince* (Hello Reader! Level 3, Grades 1 & 2). New York: Cartwheel, 1993.

Trivizas, Eugene. *The Three Little Wolves and the Big Bad Pig*. New York: Aladdin, 1997.

Ueno, Noriko. *Elephant Buttons*. New York: HarperCollins, 1973.

Willems, Mo. *Don't Let the Pigeon Drive the Bus!* Westport, CT: Hyperion Press, 2003.

Yolen, Jane. *How Do Dinosaurs Say I Love You?* New York: The Blue Sky Press, 2009.

# Index

# About the Author

BETSY DIAMANT-COHEN is an early childhood specialist and children's librarian. Dr. Diamant-Cohen has written *Mother Goose on the Loose: A Handbook and CD-ROM Kit with Scripts, Rhymes, Songs, Flannel-Board Patterns, and Activities; Booktalking Bonanza: Ten Ready-to-Use Multimedia Sessions for the Busy Librarian; Early Literacy Programming en Español: Mother Goose on the Loose Programs for Bilingual Learners;* and *The Early Literacy Kit: A Handbook and Tip Cards.*